Oldtimer Said

Oldtimer Said

Twelve Step Inspiration

Oldtimer

OLDTIMER SAID
Twelve Step Inspiration

iUniverse books may be ordered through booksellers or by contacting:

iUniverse
1663 Liberty Drive
Bloomington, IN 47403
www.iuniverse.com
844-349-9409

Author Credit: Jerome M. Oakley

ISBN: 978-1-6632-2291-6 (sc)
ISBN: 978-1-6632-2292-3 (e)

Library of Congress Control Number: 2021913234

Print information available on the last page.

iUniverse rev. date: 06/29/2021

This book is dedicated to the oldtimers who helped this addict to grasp and develop a program of recovery that saved my life. In turn, I have passed on their experience, strength and hope to hundreds of alcoholics and addicts, who have also recovered from a fatal disease.

The wisdom of those oldtimers who helped me, and the wisdom of AA Founders, is reflected in this book. Though they are no longer in the meetings, I offer the wisdom they shared with me to those who enter the rooms of recovery looking for a solution to a deadly illness.

It is hoped that these words of inspiration will move alcoholics and addicts of all type to accept the spiritual solution the Twelve Steps have provided for millions in various fellowships. Regardless of the substance we used in our addiction, the Steps offer a solution to those willing to go to any lengths to recover from a hopeless state of mind and body.

The spirituality of the Steps is only a suggested program. The pages in this book are inspired by the Big Book of Alcoholics Anonymous. Do not be discouraged by the title if you are an addict. Though the Big Book was written by alcoholics for alcoholics, time has proven that the clear-cut directions they provide have been proven to work for addicts trapped in addiction.

It is my sincere hope that these words may inspire newcomers to grasp and develop the Twelve Step program that has helped so many to recover.

May your Higher Power bless you and keep you on your journey to recovery.

Alcohol gave us a magical experience that transformed into a voodoo curse

Oldtimer said, "Cunning, baffling, powerful! This description of alcohol fits the alcoholic perfectly. This liquid, in whatever form it takes, has the power to not only transform our lives, but carries an immense power to destroy our lives. This is not so with non-alcoholics, who can take a drink without the terrible consequences alcoholics suffer. In fact, they can take it or leave it alone. They do not have to go to meetings, or work Steps, to stay sober. They are not powerless over alcohol. But for drinkers of the alcoholic persuasion, alcohol affects us to our core. It rearranged our ideas, emotions and attitudes into a whirlwind of delusion and insanity. It became a power greater than ourselves to which we surrendered our will and our lives, for it did for us what no other earthly power could accomplish. When we took that first drink of alcohol we had a sense of freedom and happiness. We lost our regret and remorse. We were overcome with a sense of peace and serenity. We felt our self esteem rise, lost our feelings of inadequacy and gained a sense of usefulness to others. We lost interest in selfish things and gained interest in in our fellows. Self-seeking slipped away. Our whole attitude and outlook upon life changed. Fear of people and economic insecurity left us. Where we were once confused, we suddenly knew how to handle situations that used to baffle us. Alcohol did for us what we could not do ourselves. This was the magic of alcohol. But over time, the script flipped and we begin to have trouble with personal relationships. We couldn't control our emotional nature. We were a prey to misery and depression. We couldn't make a living. We were consumed with a sense of uselessness. We were full of fear. We were unhappy. We couldn't be of real help to other people. Terror, bewilderment, frustration and despair became our constant companion.

This transformation is complete when we arrive in the rooms of recovery in a state of pitiful and incomprehensible demoralization. We learned that the power of alcohol was greater than any human power we could muster, and that our salvation rested with the One who has all power. That One is God, and we must find Him now! For only God has the power to reverse the damage done to us as a result of making alcohol a false idol we placed before Him. We had enshrined King Alcohol and served as its minion. Now we pledge allegiance to God and become an agent for His glory. As a result, we are blessed with His Grace, our lives are redeemed, we are restored to sanity and transformed in way that is indeed miraculous. We walk a path to freedom and happiness, so long as we remain close to God and perform His work well."

The spiritual life provides an effective mental defense against the first drink

Oldtimer said, "Alcoholics lack an effective mental defense against the first drink. We cannot think our way through the drink and make the logical decision that alcohol is destroying our lives and the lives of our loved ones. Rational thinking, common sense, self-knowledge and self-will fail to move the alcoholic away from the idea of taking the first drink-a drink that opens the door to the maniacal consumption of alcohol driven by the phenomenon of craving.

This is something that only alcoholics experience. Not even the pain, suffering and humiliation of our last drinking spree can provide a sufficient defense against the insanity of the first drink. The horrific experience that alcohol caused lodges in our temporary memory and fades away over time. However, the pleasure alcohol brought us is lodged in our permanent memory, and it is the pursuit of this pleasure that brings about every return to drinking. This is how the delusional alcoholic mind works. Non-alcoholics can use reason, logic, common sense and rational thinking to moderate their drinking, or stop altogether. Self-will and self-knowledge provides an effective mental defense for non-alcoholics. They may even have grave emotional and mental disorders, but they have an effective mental defense that provides them power over alcohol. They do not need to trust God, clean house, and help others in order to enforce their desire to remain abstinent from alcohol. They haven't a need for the self-searching, leveling of their pride and confession of their shortcomings that is required to bring about the psychic change that is necessary for the alcoholic to abstain from drinking. Non-alcoholics have an effective mental defense that works every time. With the alcoholic, there are times when our mental defense against the drink works, but there inevitably comes a certain time when that defense fails to hold our obsession for alcohol in check. This is the baffling nature of alcoholism. Sometimes human power works to keep us dry. But inevitably, there comes a time when we drink against our own will.

If we are to find permanent sobriety, our recovery must be grounded in Infinite Power. There is One who has this power. That One is God. We must find Him before that certain time falls upon us and returns us to the terror, bewilderment, frustration and despair that drinking now brings us.

In following Good Orderly Directions we channel the power of God, and it manifest into a psychic change that transforms our minds and affords us the ability to see and act on the truth about alcohol. When we fully allow this power to flow into our lives, we find that we have the elements of living that solves all of our problems and brings much of Heaven into our lives."

We turn our will and life over to God by pursuing the truth

Oldtimer said, "The only absolute truth we can know is that of our own experience. Everything else is questionable, no matter the source from which it flows. So we seek the truth of our experience with alcohol, ourselves, and others. In seeking this truth, we learn our failure in these relationships had one common element: our lack of a relationship with God. This truth led to the realization that His absence left us to our own devices, and fear dominated our lives. We often drank to overcome fear and then became fearful of a life without alcohol. We feared rejection and abandonment and sought to control and manipulate the people we cared for, only to see them reject and abandon us and our fear driven effort to control them. But, most of all, we feared taking an honest look at ourselves, for we knew in our hearts that what we had created with our life was far from the thing of beauty we had intended.

Once alcohol stops working, we have the rude awakening that alcohol was merely a symptom of a much larger problem.

Now that it could no longer cover the deficiencies in our character, we had but two choices; accept our fate as an ugly alcoholic creature and proceed to the gates of insanity and death, or live on a spiritual basis. Unfortunately, we found change was impossible without the aid of a Power greater than ourselves. At first, AA was this power. The hope we experienced when the AA fellowship welcomed us dispelled the notion that we were beyond redemption. **H**earing **O**ther **P**eople's **E**xperience of their failure with life on alcohol's terms, and their recovery from it, gave us hope that we, too, had a chance at redemption. By aligning ourselves with a **G**roup **O**f **D**runks, we **H**ad **O**ur **P**ower **E**xtended to a degree that we could accept the basic tenets of a God-centered life rooted in the truth of our failure to live without Him.

In order to achieve the necessary level of truth to affect a permanent change, we had to be truthful about our understanding of God. Thorough honesty is a requirement of a healthy relationship with God. For too long we had relied on other people's perception of God and found only failure.

To access God's Power we must access our truth. And in doing so, we gain access to God's power, so long as we remain on this axis of truth. In this way, we build the life we intended by building, first and foremost, a trusting relationship with God based on the truth as we understand it."

Inventory is the spiritual power that brings light to the truth of our psychological deformity

Oldtimer said, "Inventory isn't merely a psychological exercise that gives us clues about our character, and reveals repeated patterns of behavior that led to our downfall. It works in conjunction with our prayer and meditation life to effectively remove the layers of ego that block us off from God's Power. As we identify our resentments, fears and shame, we ask God for help in removing these barriers. If we do not know what they are, and how they negatively impact our lives, we are not likely to ask to have these defects of character removed. Our recovery from alcoholism not only requires us to detox our body from the drink, it also requires us to detox our mind from selfishness, dishonesty, resentment and fear. These are the maladies of a restless spirit that keeps us irritable and discontented with life on life's terms. And it is this agitated state of being that drives us to seek the ease and comfort that comes by taking a few drinks-drinks that eventually sends us into a state of pitiful and incomprehensible demoralization.

When these spiritual maladies are overcome, we straighten out mentally, emotionally and physically. Recovery, like alcoholism, is an inside job. Therefore, we must uncover, discover and discard that within us that keeps us walking in the valley of the shadow of death. Alcoholics are notorious for hiding a bad motive behind a good action, and it is only through rigorous honesty about our motives that we can uncover our shortcomings that lead to the first drink of a spree. Their removal requires a selfless approach to prayer.

Selfless prayer proves most effective in producing a spiritual experience that will rearrange our motives and align them with God's will. We may appear to act selfishly towards others when we place our recovery before other obligations, but God's primary will for the alcoholic is sobriety. As long as this remains our primary purpose, God's will becomes the motive for the actions we undertake. In doing so, we gain humility and find a hidden strength that remained so elusive to us in our previous prideful pursuit of power.

Through humility we bring balance into our life. It is hard to stumble when you fall to your knees in prayer. No man stands as tall as when he kneels before His Creator. When we do so our past becomes His property and we are free of the grasp of the selfishness, dishonesty, resentments, fears and shame that dogged us for so many years. Now can we begin to live life happy, joyous and free in a fourth dimension of existence of which we had never dreamed."

Uncover, discover and discard the shame that binds us to alcohol

Oldtimer said, "Step Four requires us to proceed immediately into Step Five. We have a written inventory that has opened wounds from our past. Delay is deadly, for we have brought into our consciousness our past actions that carry the burden of shame. Our secrets have been uncovered in the privacy of our inventory. Next comes the discovery phase in the Fifth Step, where we expose them to another human being. This is followed by a willingness to discard the defects of character we have uncovered in our inventory. As with any physical wound, we must close the psychic wounds we uncovered in the Fourth Step before they become infected. The longer we linger on the wreckage of the past, the more damage it does to our self-esteem, emotional security, and psychological integrity. We must confess our wrongs at the first opportunity. We admit them to God for forgiveness, to ourselves for acceptance, and to another human being for humility.

In our First Step experience we acknowledge our powerlessness over alcohol. In Step Two we accepted only God's power could restore us to sanity. And in Step Three we committed ourselves to go to any lengths for victory over alcohol by following God's way of life. Now we are embarking on a new relationship with our Creator that will restore us to sanity and right living with society.

As a result of our maniacal drinking, we became outright mental defectives in full flight from reality and maladjusted to life. Only when we become grounded in God's power are we restored to sanity and able to adjust to life on life's terms without the aid of a drink. Through Step Five we remove the fear that binds us to shame and blocks us off from the Power we need to recover from a hopeless state of mind and body. When this happens our fear falls from us and we begin to feel the nearness God's presence. This spiritual experience is the beginning of the end of our desire for alcohol. Our nearness to the Sunlight of the Spirit burns from our consciousness the shame that feeds our obsession to drink, and initiates a life-long process of character reconstruction that will result in peace, happiness, and joy in limitless measure."

Spiritual growth hinges upon our willingness to change

Oldtimer said, "Steps Six and Seven are an attitude adjustment that propels us into the remaining Steps. In Step Six we adopt an attitude of willingness to let go of the defects of character that feed our obsession and makes our life unmanageable. In Step Seven, we humbly accept ourselves as we are and present ourselves to God as we are to serve Him and our fellow man. This humility allows the truth to take root in our consciousness that it might overcome the False Evidence Appearing Real that often blocks our spiritual growth. It is these attitudes that direct our prayer life.

Prayer is an effective agent of change for the alcoholic whose hope is the growth and maintenance of a spiritual life. When we fall short of God's chosen plan for our lives, we turn to our list of defects and ask God to remove from our character that which is blocking us from executing His will. Very often it is fear that blocks our growth. Self-centered fear is a chameleon the morphs into different manifestations of self, such as pride, shame, selfishness, dishonesty and resentment. Therefore, the proper use of prayer for the alcoholic should be the fear prayer.

How often have we misrepresented ourselves for fear of what others would think of us were the truth known? Our fear of exposure to the truth about ourselves keeps many alcoholics from the confession required in the Fifth Step. As a result, they return to the bottle. How many of us have felt the trepidation of making amends and exposing ourselves as a liar, cheat or a thief? When we balk at a Step, it is the False Evidence Appearing Real that is at the root of our reluctance to follow through with our Third Step commitment, where we develop a willingness to let loose of the pride that leads us to death's embrace. Until we do so we are dishonest with ourselves and God on the deepest level of our being.

Fortunately, we need only make spiritual progress. God loved us at our worst because He knew it was the best we could do. Therefore, we have no reason to fear His judgement. We offered our best and worst to Him in Step Seven and the case was dismissed when He accepted us, and entrusted us, as agents for the advancement of His Creation."

Our Creator accepts us as we are so that we might become all we can be

Oldtimer said, **"My Creator, I am now willing that you should have all of me, good and bad."**

We have uncovered the flaws in our make up that lead to an unmanageable life and makes the thought drinking attractive option. Now we offer ourselves, flaws and all, to God, as we now experience God. We made this decision on faith in Step Three, but now we begin to have a spiritual experience, and have moved beyond faith into a deeper relationship with God, with the understanding that He loves us at our worst because He knows it is the best we can do.

"I pray you now remove from me every single defect of character, which stands in the way of my usefulness to you and my fellows."

We know God much better, thanks to our work with the previous Steps. And with this knowledge, we come to trust that He knows what is best for our spiritual growth. In our new relationship with our Creator, no weapon formed against us shall prosper. Even in the worst situation, we emerge from it without a desire for a drink, and we are blessed with either a lesson or a blessing that increases our effectiveness at helping others to recover.

"Grant me strength as I go forward from here to do your bidding."

Strength means power! Now, in all of our affairs, we will have the power to live up to our moral and philosophical convictions. We carried a great deal of shame because we went against what we knew to be moral, just, and right. We now understand that our drinking is an act of self-destruction. But with God's power at our disposal, we will be able to resist the temptation to fall into the alcoholic trap. We will be able to see and act on the truth, rather than believe the lie that alcohol will do something for us. This Power we seek will also enable us to go forward with the amends process.

Many of us looked at Step Nine when we came into the rooms and balked at the very idea of making amends. "What an order! I can't go through with it," we may have exclaimed. This is true. But after Step Seven, we are no longer alone in our endeavor to stay sober. God does with us what we could never do alone. He is our able and willing partner on the path to our happy destiny."

Willing to make amends means willing to forgive

Oldtimer said, "When we thoroughly review our amends list we need to consider not only those we owe an amends, but also what forgiveness is necessary on our part. Hurt people hurt people, and we have determined that those who hurt us were, perhaps, spiritually sick. We pray that we might be helpful to them, and ask for knowledge of God's will in the affair. Until we have truly forgiven those who have harmed us, we will not be able to place out of our minds the wrongs they have done to us, and we will continue to be tortured with a restlessness born of vengeance. This is a luxury for normal people that we alcoholics can ill afford. Vengeance leads to hate. Hate leads to anger. Anger leads to resentment. Resentment leads to stinking thinking. Stinking thinking leads to stinking drinking. Stinking drinking leads to jails, institutions and death.

Our readiness to forgive determines whether we are entirely ready to make complete amends to those who had <u>harmed us</u>. Therefore, we list our amends according to our willingness to forgive. We list those amends we are willing to make now, those we are willing to make later, those amends we may, or may not, be willing to make, and those we are never going to make. For the most difficult amends, we need to pray for God's will for us in each matter, and ask for the willingness to forgive them. We do not forgive them solely for their benefit. We forgive them for our benefit as well. We deserve the peace that forgiveness brings. When we forgive our transgressors, we remove the noose of victimhood that we placed around our neck, and find victory in God's grace.

God forgives us as we forgive others. We will find that as we forgive, we are blessed with grace, and come to know that we are worthy of the freedom and peace forgiveness brings. As we work our amends list, we come to realize that those we have balked at making amends with offer us the greatest freedom, peace and serenity.

We now have a new value system. For we are now living in God's economy. And once we make our peace of mind non-negotiable, the willingness to forgive the unforgivable becomes a purpose we strive towards. When this happens, we can truly say that we are free. Free to love, free to live and free to forgive. For we are truly living in the image of our Creator!"

Living the Steps is our living amends

Oldtimer said, "Amends means change, and the AA way of life brings about a change in our personality sufficient to overcome alcoholism. There may be some people on our Eighth Step list that we cannot, or should not, make direct amends. We should stand ready if the opportunity arises, but in the meantime, we continue to change the way we live so as not to repeat the offensive behavior that brought about harm to others.

Alcoholics have long sought the easier, softer way in life. Seeking our comfort nearly led us to a comfortable grave. The living amends that we must make, if we expect to live long and happily in this life, is to remain sober. Steps Ten, Eleven and Twelve is the easier, softer way that insures our sobriety. Good comes to us cloaked in hard work. But soon the hard work becomes a habit, and we are left only with the fruit of our good work.

The spiritual life is not a theory. It is something we must work toward one day at a time. We must live the AA way of life on a daily basis, or return to the way of death that delivered us to a state of pitiful, incomprehensible demoralization. In Step Ten, we continue to take personal inventory. This is crucial for the delusional alcoholic mind that has made a fine art of denial. As we grow more comfortable with feeling uncomfortable, our capacity to accept the truth increases. We move from a state of denial to a state of rigorous honesty. We may never become perfectly honest, but awareness of our dishonesty does allow us to make amends for the harm it has brought about. And in doing so, we increase our comfort with the truth and continue to grow spiritually. This change in our relationship with the truth will set us free, but first it is going to hurt us.

Our First Step experience with alcohol proved this to be true. Until the pain of our drinking became stronger than the pain of not drinking, we continued to drink. And until the pain of sobriety became greater than the pain of change the Steps require, we remained trapped in the revolving door of relapse, going in and out of the rooms of recovery until we found the comfort of the grave that alcohol's way of death always delivers. Through prayer and meditation, we improve our conscious contact with God, and receive the power to transcend our pain and transform it into our gain. We find that no weapon the alcoholic ego marshals against our recovery prospers.

Our humiliation is transformed into humility once we walk through the pain of the truth we have denied for so long. And it is this experience with the truth that allows us to be rigorously honest when carrying the message to the sick and suffering alcoholic. This pain we carry is diminished when we share it with the alcoholic in need of our experience, strength, and hope. We suddenly realize that the pain we walked through has a purpose. Nothing is wasted in God's economy. Even pain has value when we fit ourselves to be of maximum service to God and the people about us. It becomes the taproot of our spiritual growth, so long as we continue to make amends by living the AA way of life."

We continue to watch our words, thoughts and motives

Oldtimer said, "Our thoughts become our words. Our words become our actions. Our actions become our habits. Our habits become our life. In Step Ten, we begin the discipline of watching our thoughts and actions. We watch for the thoughts that originate in the ego, and germinate in the soil of our alcoholic mind. Whenever we follow through with these thoughts, and put them into action, we have **E**ased **G**od **O**ut and have stepped from the high road that leads to our happy destiny.

We continue to watch our thoughts, words and actions for selfishness. When we are thinking of ourself, first and only, we open the door for our old alcoholic behaviors to manifest in our life once again. We continue to watch for our fears which lead to the delusional thinking that makes **F**alse **E**vidence **A**ppear **R**eal. In this state, we lapse into paralysis analysis, and procrastinate on our program of spiritual growth. We continue to watch for resentments—a dangerous state of mind that has destroyed a multitude of alcoholics. We continue to watch for dishonesty and the little lies we tell ourselves which eventually leads to the big lie that precedes every relapse—"It will be different this time."

Through this practice of watching, we begin to take notice of the manifestations of self that emanates from our instincts for sex, society, and security. As we continue to develop this habit, we also take note of our intuitive thoughts that increases as we decrease our response to thoughts rooted in our instincts. We no longer react to life, but instead act upon it as agents of God who live in service to Him and our fellow man. It is through maximum service, where we play the role God assigns, that we are able rise above the fatal selfishness that creates the stinking thinking that always leads to stinking drinking. Through the discipline of watching we learn to move out of self-will and clear the path to enter the World of the Spirit. We develop a deeper relationship with God that allows us to more easily determine instinctive thoughts from intuitive thoughts. In this state, our lives begin to change for the better. For we are no longer transformed by the world, but are transformed by the Spirit. A transformation that is evidenced when those around us find their lives improving as we continue to grow spiritually. We are no longer a tornado roaring through their lives, but a soothing breeze and a sunlit sky that lights up their world."

Prayer is the key that liberates us from bondage to our alcoholic mind

Oldtimer said, "Alcoholics Anonymous offers the sick and suffering alcoholic a spiritual program of action that will release us from bondage to our alcoholic mind, and one day at a time, grant us a reprieve from our fatal malady. Selfishness and self-centeredness is at the root of our problems. We Ease God Out and think only of our wants, motives, demands and desires. This reckless pursuit of pleasure leads us to obsessive behavior that paves the way to every alcoholic spree and the calamity that follows.

In the Steps, we make conscious contact with God. Through the combination of prayer and the prescribed actions, do we trudge the road to a happy destiny.

In Step Four, we pray for release from resentment and fear, and ask God how to correct the harms we have perpetrated upon His world. In Step Five we express thanks that we know Him better. In Step Six we pray for the willingness to be willing to let go and let God when we hold too tightly to our character defects. In Step Seven, we pray God remove from us the defects of character that do not serve His purpose, and grant us the strength to serve Him and our fellow man. In Steps Eight and Nine, we once again pray for willingness and the strength to do the right thing.

In learning the AA way of life, we have adjusted our attitude toward prayer. No longer do we selfishly pray for external rewards, but instead pray for an internal transformation that helps us to better accept life on life's terms, and achieve the peace of mind we once found in the drink. Thus have we prepared ourselves for the proper use of prayer, that when combined with our continued use of inventory, sets us free from those maladies which bedevil us and manufacture all sorts of misery in our life. Through selfless prayer, our conscious contact with God improves. And as we act to remove those defects of character that block us off from God, we increase our effectiveness with meditation and better understand God's will for us. When we drew near Him, He revealed Himself to us in the face of our fellow travelers on the road to a happy destiny."

God's power flows through open channels

Oldtimer said, "The Twelve Steps are a power move designed to remove the spiritual blocks between alcoholics and God. We suffer from a hopeless state of mind and body that places us beyond human aid. Frothy emotional appeal from our loved ones fail to provide the necessary motivation to drive us away from the drink. The warning of a doctor of an impending health crisis caused by our drinking proves an insufficient force in our battle against the bottle. Nor does a geographical change provide a remedy to our fatal malady.

With the alcoholic, there is a complete failure of the survival instinct. The instinct that keeps us from putting our hand on a hot stove utterly fails to stop our drinking. We have an obsession of the mind so great that it drive us to drink against our will. There is One that has the power we need to recover. Only God can provide us an effective defense against the first drink.

A spiritual awakening brings us a connection with God, and through this connection we receive the power we need to overcome our obsession for alcohol. This power has always been available to us, but only when we come to believe in the hopelessness and futility of life as we have been living it, do we attain the willingness to begin the self-searching, the leveling of our pride and the confession of our shortcomings which opens the channel to God's power.

We have to keep that connection clear by following the disciplines of Steps Ten, Eleven, and Twelve. We continue to watch for the spiritual maladies that block us from God. Selfishness, dishonesty, resentment, and fear are fuel to the mental obsession. When they crop up we ask God to remove them at once. We talk to someone immediately about it, and make amends quickly if we have harmed anyone.

In Step Eleven, we seek through prayer and meditation to gain knowledge of God's will for us and the power to carry it out. If we sense a loss of His power in our life it is probably because we are going places God doesn't want us to go, seeing people God doesn't want us to see, and doing things God doesn't want us to do. When we live in His will we receive the power we need to recover.

In Step Twelve, we transmit this power to others. We continue to practice the principles of power in all of our affairs, and carry the message to another alcoholic. When two are gathered in His name, doing His work, God provides what we need and we sense the flow of His Spirit into us."

Our alcoholic mind is out to get us

Oldtimer said, "As alcoholics we must come to understand and accept that our mind is out to get us. If we expect to recover from a hopeless state of mind and body, and live long and happily in this world, we must treat the source of our illness, not merely the symptom. We must uncover, discover and discard the causes and conditions that leads to our obsession to consume that which is consuming us.

We have a body that can't take alcohol, and a mind that won't leave it alone. Underlying our sound reasoning and logic lies the subtle insanity of the first drink. In this state of pre-lapse every thought we have stems from an alcoholic mind. This is the thinking that leads us to the idea of controlling our drinking, and brings us a step closer to the next relapse. Only when we give up on our thinking do we come to believe that a Power greater than ourselves can restore us to sanity. And only through the pain of drinking do we give up on our thinking and fully accept the nature of our problem.

We don't have a drinking problem as much as we have a thinking problem. We think we can safely drink. And only when we make a decision to turn our will and life over to the **G**ood **O**rderly **D**irections of the Steps, can it be said that we have come to accept the hopelessness and futility of life as we had been living it. This thought brings us to the self-searching process that levels our pride and enables us to humbly confess our shortcomings.

We can't beat alcohol. God can beat alcohol. We cease fighting the drink, and allow Him to do for us what we can not do for ourselves. When we completely give up on ourselves and surrender to God, we are amazed at the grace that delivers us from the evil of alcohol that held us in bondage to it's way of death.

With each Step we take, we no longer follow the low road to the gates of insanity and death. Instead we take the high road to the spiritual realm, and begin to trudge our way to a happy destiny."

Deflation of the ego leads to a psychic change

Oldtimer said, "The alcoholic ego is very different from the average ego. It is why alcohol is cunning, baffling and powerful to the alcoholic and why we remain under the influence of alcohol long after we quit drinking. We can go through the most horrific events that would psychologically and emotionally devastate other people, yet we bounce back from it in a few days as though nothing had ever happened. This is why people are amazed when we return to drinking after another alcoholic spree that ended in disaster.

Based on their reality, the disaster should have been sufficient to make us give up drinking forever. But the ever-resilient alcoholic ego balks at the idea of such surrender. It is a kamikaze pilot driven to bring the alcoholic to their complete and utter destruction. This is why every alcoholic must hit bottom and accept the horrifying reality that their mind is out to get them. Unless we undergo an entire psychic change, we remain under the influence of alcohol and a danger to ourselves and the people about us.

This psychic change can only occur when there is complete deflation of the alcoholic ego. Therefore, it is essential that the newcomer launch into the Steps while their ego is in a subdued state. This only occurs after a crisis that the alcoholic cannot evade, or explain away.

Once it rebuilds, the alcoholic ego is highly resistant to change. This is why newcomers come into the rooms in a surrendered state, but after a short time are emboldened to return to drinking. Even if they do not drink for a period of time, they are not likely to work the Steps necessary to bring about the much-needed psychic change.

The Steps are designed to reduce the grasp that the ego has on our mind. This is not an overnight matter. It is a lifetime endeavor, for the alcoholic ego, once dethroned as ruler of our mind, continually works to **E**ase **G**od **O**ut and reclaim it's former exalted status. Only by living the AA way of life do we keep the ego reduced to it's proper size and allow ourselves to live free and sober in accordance with God's will."

God's will for the sick and suffering alcoholic is the Steps

Old timers said, "Until we come to the end of self, we will not surrender our will and life to God and His perfect will. We first experience this end of self when we hit bottom in Step One. It is only under these most dire circumstances, that we admit to ourselves that we are nothing, and are prepared to surrender to God's way of life. We further experience this in recovery when we hit bottom in our sex life, emotional life, material life, financial life and spiritual life.

Our old ideas, emotions and attitudes that govern us are based on our outsized instincts for sex, society and security. Even after we surrender they remain in our mind and direct our behavior. Only when we encounter a crisis as a result of following these emotionally defective impulses do we become willing to let go of them, and fully accept God's way of life. This is why we seek spiritual progress, not spiritual perfection. Our aim is for spiritually perfect ideas, for only in doing so do we expose our human limitations and shortcomings.

Success at changing our behavior only comes through the failures that produce enough pain to create the willingness we need to affect a change in our approach to life. In AA, we fail our way to success. The Steps are a spiritual process that lead to certain success only after repeated failures. As we continue to hit new bottoms as a result of living on our will, we open ourselves to a deeper surrender of our will and lives over to God and His perfect will.

Each of the Twelve Steps is a surrender to God's will. If we resist applying them to our life, our old behaviors persist in all of our affairs. We find we are powerless over these behaviors that arise out of our character defects, and only through the aid of a Power greater than self can we change. Only when we are sick and tired of being sick and tired of our old behaviors will we let go and let God take us to a more abundant life.",

In God's will is the freedom from bondage to alcohol

Oldtimer said, "Our relief from bondage to self begins with prayer and proceeds into inventory, where we identify our specific defects of character and pray for release from the old ideas, emotions and attitudes that pollute our relations with God and our fellow man. We pray for those we resent: "God, this is a sick person. How can I be helpful to them? God, save me from being angry. Thy will be done.""

With this prayer, we broaden our perception of others, based on our new perception of ourselves as spiritually sick people. We understand that they, like ourselves, are spiritually sick. We find through inventory that we hurt others because we ourselves have been hurt. So it is with those who harm us. Hurt people simply hurt people.

Our Third Step commitment to serve God is immediately challenged, as we pray for knowledge of how we may be of service to our fellow spiritual sufferer. This empathy reflects a new attitude for the self-centered alcoholic, and only through prayer will we find the power to act upon this new attitude. We then acknowledge to God that we need His help to save us from ourselves. Anger is a dubious luxury for normal men. But in the mind of the alcoholic, it is as poisonous as a drink. So we seek only to do God's will, not our own. We find salvation in loving our enemy as ourselves.

In some cases, there is immediate release from the resentment. But with deep-rooted resentments, we **P**ray **U**ntil **S**omething **H**appens. At the root of our resentments, we find fear. We fear we may lose something we possess, so we became angry and recycled that fear into a resentment. Or maybe we felt threatened and feared we would lose something we cherished, and once again, anger dominated our mind. So we pray: "God remove my fear and direct my attention to what you would have me be."

Our sick mind is far too twisted to escape the double edged sword of resentment and fear with our own power. But God could and would remove these defects, if we sought, above all else, to do His will. For it is in God's will that we find freedom from our bondage to the poison of alcohol which carries fatal consequences for us, and our bondage to self which makes our life unmanageable.

In His will we no longer are creators of chaos and confusion, but act as an instrument of His peace. As such, we bring peace and harmony into the lives of those we encounter, so long as we live in His will."

A new relationship with our Creator brings forth a new and wonderful life

Oldtimer said, "In Step Five, we are trying to develop a new relationship with our Creator because our old relationship held insufficient power to win the battle against alcohol. Even religious alcoholic have to admit the shortcomings in their relationship with God. If it were sufficient they would not drink. If they have taken this vital and crucial Step, it is an acceptance of the shortcomings in their spiritual condition. For atheist and agnostics these shortcomings are very apparent, but every alcoholic who surrenders to the need for confession acknowledges their personal need for the power God offers.

We have listed the flaws in our make up that blocks the power we need from entering our lives. With selfishness, dishonesty, resentment, and fear, we have taken ourselves hostage and barricaded the door through which God enters. It is up to us to remove uncover, discover, and discard these obstacles.

God is gracious and only enters where we invite Him. When we take the Fifth Step, we admit our deeper need for God by confessing our wrongs that we may receive His forgiveness. In accepting His forgiveness, we open the door for Him to enter our heart and mind so that He can begin the necessary transformation that will free us from our bondage to alcohol. Where His light shines the purity of His love flows and brings healing from the guilt, shame, remorse and regret that weighs down our spirit and drives us to lift our spirits with alcohol.

When our spirit rises to meet God, the partnership we formed with God in the Third Step begins to blossom. As a result, we are empowered in our recovery to act as His agents and advance His Creation. Our sobriety acts as a demonstration of His omnipotence, and we demonstrate His love, His power, and His way of life to those alcoholics we would help to recover from a hopeless state of mind and body. We become the depth and weight of the AA message and the mercy, grace and redemption God offers to alcoholics who earnestly seek Him."

Willingness is essential to our spiritual resurrection from the alcoholic pit

Oldtimer said, "Step Six is a stepping stone to Step Eleven and greater conscious contact with God. As we move on from this Step and work our way through the others, we arrive at Step Eleven with a willingness to work in earnest to improve our relationship God through prayer and meditation.

This is a process that began with prayer in Step Three, and continued to develop with prayer in the Steps that preceded the Eleventh Step. Through this process, we strengthened our spiritual nature through inventory, confession and courage to change by making the necessary amends we uncovered in the learning phase of the AA way of life. As this happened we underwent a spiritual transformation that left us uncomfortable with our character defects. And as a people accustomed to seeking their own comfort above everything else, we now find that doing so carries with it a great price.

Our freedom from bondage requires us to become willing to let loose of the defects of character that now make us uncomfortable with God's will. Pride very often gets in the way of us releasing these detrimental defects, because it convinces us that the pain of letting them go is far greater than the pain of holding on to them. To overcome this pride we must step out on faith and ask God to remove this fatal shortcoming. Pride is a manifestation of the ego, and the ego is opposed to our spiritual development. It does not want us to change. Its desire is to keep control of our thought life and continue to **E**ase **G**od **O**ut of our affairs.

The attitude of willingness we adopted in Step Six is essential to our freedom from bondage to the past. It is in the past that the ego draws its power. Through our prayer life and meditation life we dethrone the ego, focus our thought life in the present, and allow the Sunlight of the Spirit to reign supreme in our mind. It is our thought life that will direct the actions we take from this point forward.

By expanding and enlarging our spiritual life, we are rocketed into the fourth dimension which gets infinitely more wonderful as time passes. As we perfect our spiritual life, we become effective servants to God and the people about us, and it is in this service that we grow into the image of our Creator."

Where God guides He provides

Oldtimer said, "Grant me strength as I go forward from here to do your bidding."

Step Seven is when we open our lives to God's power. We have done much to remove the defects of character which stand in the way of our usefulness to God. We have admitted the weak items in our character, and now we find in our weakness is God's strength perfected.

We often hear alcoholics proclaim they are powerless over people, places, and things. This is likely so because they are going places God did not intend for them to go, doing things God not intend for them to do with people God did not intend to be in their life. In doing His bidding we may need to change our playmates, playgrounds and playthings. We walk a new road as an alcoholic transformed by the Spirit, so we leave behind our childish ways and make progress towards spiritual maturity.

We are granted the power to be successful when we seek to do God's will over our own. However, our vision of success may be quite different from God's vision. His vision is for the restoration of our soul. Very often, our vision of success lies in the material realm. When we practice spiritual principles in all of our affairs, a healing power flows into our life. We find that in God's economy no experience is wasted, and we grow through even the most difficult of times. We will receive a lesson or a blessing that will be helpful to another alcoholic in the future.

We are God's agents and when our actions reflect His will, success is destined to follow. So long as we stay close to him and perform His work well, we live life more abundantly. In doing His bidding, our defects may sometimes be useful. The Deadly Sins of pride, anger, greed, gluttony, envy, lust and sloth actually become valuable teachers of the Cardinal Virtues prudence, temperance, fortitude, justice, faith, hope, charity. For in doing God's bidding, the virtuous road is much easier to trudge, and as alcoholics we naturally seek the easier softer way.

Through the Deadly Sins, we learn what not to do. We learn that self-will is the way of death and destruction for alcoholics of our type. This is a valuable lesson that can't be taught. It must be learned. The Cardinal Virtues are the fruits of the Spirit which bring us priceless blessings that increase in value when we share them with the sick and suffering alcoholic."

Forgiveness brings us freedom from pride and ego

Oldtimer said, "When we make a list of people we have harmed, it is a blow to our alcoholic ego and a major step into humility. To admit we are wrong feels like death to the ego and separates it from one of its most deadly weapons— pride. This deadly sin blinds us to the truth and binds us to the alcohol.

Pride is a dubious luxury for normal people, but for the alcoholic it is as deadly as the drink. Our pride suffers in the light of the truth. When we experience inventory, we have swallowed a big chunk of truth about ourselves. We thought we were only hurting ourselves with our drinking, and if we harmed anyone, they deserved our wrath.

In Steps Four and Five, our delusions are brought into focus, and the truth dispels the notion of our innocence in our most troubling affairs. As we acknowledge our actions that stem from our character defects, and take responsibility to repair the harm we have caused others, we grow in humility and bind ourselves to God's will. More than likely, our loved ones are at the top of our amends list. For even with the best of intentions, we hurt them deeply. They placed their trust in us, and we repeatedly violated their trust with our maniacal drinking habit. We hurt them so deeply that a simple apology proves insufficient. If we are to rebuild the sweet relationships we have damaged, we must change the nature of our character. And we can do this only if we adopt God's purpose for our lives, and fit ourselves for maximum service to Him and our fellow man.

Our Eighth Step list confirms that when we act upon our will, we are weapons of mass destruction. As such, it provides greater motivation to carry forth with God's will, make complete amends to those we have harmed, and repair all that we have destroyed. Over time, we harvest the fruits of our labors, and the nature of our newfound relationship with our Creator is reflected in our relationship with those in our orbit."

Spiritual growth gives us a new pair of glasses

Oldtimer said, "As we grow spiritually, our perception of ourselves and the impact we have on others changes. The third column of the resentment inventory points out how the harms others inflicted upon us transformed us into a vessel fit for a drink. Our freedom from the bottle lies in our willingness to forgive our transgressors and make amends for the harms we have caused. Therefore, we take a hard, honest look at whose self-esteem we have harmed, whose emotional and material security have we harmed, whose emotional and material ambitions have we harmed, and whose personal and sexual relations we have threatened or interfered with.

Hurt people hurt people, and we alcoholics freely transmitted the pain we received from others. The golden rule of alcoholism is do unto others as others have done unto you. In our delusional mind, our victim status qualifies us to become predatory in our actions towards others. So it seems to us the pain we inflicted upon others is justified by the pain we suffered at the hands of others. This pain becomes so ingrained in our psyche that sometimes we do unto others before they do unto us. In this way, we become a harbinger of pain that brings chaos and confusion into the lives of others. And when they retaliate, it reconfirms our victim status and the cycle of pain continues.

If we continue to harm others, we are quite sure to drink, so we must take action to change our nature, so that we can change the nature of our relationships. Through inventory and amends, we expose the cycle of harm and come to rely on God's will rather than our own. We bring love and forgiveness to the cycle of harm, and learn to live in harmony with our fellow man. We treat them as God would have us, even if our mind screams out for revenge.

We reap what we sow. There is no way around this spiritual law. And as long as we sow harm into the lives of others it is returned to us. When we sow goodness and light into the lives of others, that too do we reap. Sometimes quickly, sometimes slowly, the tide of life turns in our favor, so long as we make amends and plant seeds of love, forgiveness, and kindness along the path of our recovery."

Self awareness keeps our life n balance

Oldtimer said, "Step Ten is where we maintain our self-awareness. Very often we slip into our old alcoholic behaviors without realizing it. Before we know it, we are embroiled in chaos and confusion that threatens our serenity and, thus, our sobriety. It is then that we pray, in faith, for the wisdom to know what must be changed within us so we can accept that without us which disturbs us. When we rigorously practice letting go and letting God we are easily able to match calamity with serenity. So we continue to watch for the manifestations of self that bedevil us and makes our lives unmanageable.

Selfishness, dishonesty, resentment, and fear are the triggers of self that draw us back into our old alcoholic behavior. They are subtle in nature, and we often find ourselves acting out on them without our awareness. This is why we must constantly work against them by practicing their opposite virtue. On a daily basis, we practice selflessness by doing something for others and expect nothing in return. We live a life rooted in forgiveness.

Emmet Fox suggested a daily declaration of forgiveness to the world for anything ever done to us so that hidden resentments are nipped in the bud. We practice absolute honesty in our prayer life by confessing daily our sins to God, and seeking His guidance in all of our affairs. And we practice faith in Him by living according to the AA program and accepting life as it presents itself to us. Through this practice we develop awareness of our Higher Self, that which God created.

Alcoholism transformed us into a lover of things and a user of people. In the past, we may have been kind, considerate, generous, modest and self-sacrificing, but we did so expecting something in return. We weren't being kind; we were doing business. We weren't being considerate; we were doing business. We weren't being generous; we were doing business. We weren't being modest and self-sacrificing; we were doing business.

In recovery, we become a lover of people and a user of things. When we avail ourselves to spiritual principles and practice them in all of our affairs we no longer seek reward for our virtuous behavior. For virtuous behavior is a reward unto itself. It is evidence that we are no longer transformed by the world, but by the Spirit. In our selflessness, we maximize our service to others, and allow God to use us to further His plans. We no longer expect anything in return for doing His will, for the opportunity to do so is a grace we did not deserve. Thus do we become His agents, and we are empowered to help other alcoholics to achieve the miracle of recovery."

Prayer and meditation prepares us for maximum service

Oldtimer said, Prayer and meditation are essential elements of our new life if in recovery. If we are going to fit ourselves to be of maximum service to God and the people about us, we must maintain conscious contact with God.

In our Third Step decision, we placed ourselves unreservedly under God's care and direction, and began the process of fitting ourselves to serve Him and our fellow man by letting loose of our petty self-interests. In the Fourth Step, we learned to pray for our enemies, asking how we could be of service to them. We learned to overcome our fears through prayer, and to meditate for a solution to the harm we inflicted upon others.

After we cleared away the self-will that blocked us from God in our Fifth Step and drew near to Him, we expressed in prayer our gratitude that we knew Him better. With this knowledge of a God personal to us, we asked Him for the willingness to be willing to have our defects of character removed. We then prayed that God remove the defects of character that stand in the way of our usefulness to Him and our fellow man. We then prayed for the strength to go forward to do His bidding.

In Steps Eight and Nine we prayed for the willingness to make amends, and for guidance in making right our wrongs. Step Ten is a repetition of our request that God remove the defects of character when they manifest in our daily affairs. Step Eleven advises us to ask in prayer each morning for God to direct our thinking and divorce our minds from selfish, dishonest, self-seeking motives. As we go through our day, we pause when agitated (resentment) or doubtful (fear), and ask God for the right thought or action.

The more we apply prayer to the daily affairs of our life, the more wisdom and understanding we develop. As we are endowed with the Infinite Wisdom of God, we change our behavior and are blessed with an abundance of serenity that makes our conscious contact with God much more effective.

Serenity is the state of being where we are best able to hear God's voice. This intuition is increased the more we apply **G**ood **O**rderly **D**iscipline to our prayer life."

We pay our debt when we carry another alcoholic through the Steps

Oldtimer said, "As payment for a debt we can never fully repay, we pass on the priceless set of spiritual tools which brought us a spiritual awakening that released us from our destructive obsession for alcohol. When anyone anywhere reaches out, we want the hand of AA to be there offering the tools of recovery. For this we are responsible.

As alcoholics, we know it is an insufficient measure to simply stop drinking. Doing so only addresses the symptom of the underlying problem. Yet, this is what the newcomer has been hearing from non-alcoholics as the solution to their problem. They may have many problems, but these cannot be addressed until the obsession to drink is lifted. Only those who have struggled with life on life's terms, and pursued alcohol as a solution to their problem, can understand the frustration of the alcoholic who feels tortured when alcohol is taken out their life.

Unsedated reality leaves us restless, irritable and discontented until we once again seek the ease and comfort that we receive from the first drink. Unfortunately, this chemical peace of mind comes at a high price. After we take the first drink, the phenomenon of craving sets in and we are off on another alcoholic spree that brings us to a state of pitiful, incomprehensible demoralization.

As recovered alcoholics, our experience with alcoholism, and recovery from it, gives us a unique perspective because we view the problem from the inside out. When we share our alcoholic experience with the newcomer, they feel the same sense of relief that we felt when we finally met someone who understood the true nature of our alcohol problem. This experience is half of the qualification to be a sponsor. An alcoholic isn't inclined to listen to someone who hasn't had the same relationship with alcohol that they've experienced. This is the initial link in the chain that connects the newcomer to Alcoholics Anonymous. We have a common. problem, but the greater qualification to be a sponsor is our experience with the common solution, the Twelve Steps.

The sense of relief the newcomer feels on their arrival in the rooms does not spell freedom from alcoholism. It merely raises their hope for recovery from a hopeless state of mind and body. When we lead the newcomer through the Steps it is a demonstration of our faith in God's way of life, and with this demonstration we insure their recovery and ours. And it is their spiritual experience that opens us to a greater awakening in the World of the Spirit."

Lack of choice and control is the double edged sword of powerlessness

Oldtimer said, "When we show up in the rooms of recovery, we come in with a back problem. Someone is on our back about our drinking. But eventually we come to realize our real problem is we are powerless over alcohol. The only question is are we aware of it, and do we understand what it means to our life.

Yes, our life is unmanageable, and this may be our motivation for coming to AA. But this is only evidence of the overriding problem of powerlessness. What it means to be powerless is we have lost the power of choice and control when it comes to alcohol. On any given day we can't say for certain whether we will drink or not. We may have a very strong desire to not drink, but this desire provides little defense against an overpowering obsession for drink. And once we succumb to the desire for alcohol, we ignite a craving that leads us on another alcoholic spree. This double-edged sword leaves us in critical condition with a fatal illness for which man has yet to find a cure.

Unfortunately, our condition leaves us not only powerless over the consumption of alcohol, but also over our thoughts about alcohol. In spite of all the evidence we have that shows beyond a shadow of doubt that we are powerless over alcohol, our mind constantly conjures up fantasies of how we shall apply power over that which is destroying us. Our only solution to this insanity must come from a Power greater than ourselves. A Higher Power that can shine a light in the dark recesses of our mind where this insanity resides-the subconscious mind.

Man cannot affect a change on the subconscious mind, but God can and will if we seek Him on the path He has laid out for us in the Steps. Our salvation from our fatal malady lies in the spiritual life AA offers. Just as we made drinking a lifetime affair, so too must we completely give ourselves to the spiritual life. Doing so will provide an effective mental defense against the first drink, and thus do we avoid the loss of control that leads to another alcoholic spree."

Came to believe a power greater than ourselves could restore us to truth

Oldtimer said, "Spiritually bankrupt people seek pleasure to account for the lack of purpose and meaning absent from their lives. This leaves them open to an evil that comes in the form of pleasure. Alcoholics are an extreme example of this spiritual bankruptcy. We thought we had found the answer with alcohol, but our false solution only magnified our bankruptcy. We found great pleasure in alcohol, but in the end we were left with the evil of alcoholism. So ecstatic was our release from the morbidity of the reality of life on life's terms, that we were willing to go to any lengths to protect our right to drink. We thought alcohol was the answer to our spiritual bankruptcy.

For a while it worked, and we were willing to make any sacrifice necessary for the pleasure we received from this magical elixir. We blinded ourselves to reality of our descent into madness once alcohol ceased doing for us what we could not do for ourselves. We could not see and act on the truth about our relationship with alcohol.

When this insanity is complete, our spiritual bankruptcy begins to manifest in our external life, and our lives are not only unmanageable, they are unbelievable! We never imagined that our solution would lead only to a state of pitiful, incomprehensible demoralization. We were in full flight from reality, and only through a consistent and rigorous pursuit of the truth do we address our spiritual bankruptcy and restored to sanity.

The truth sets us free, but first it hurts us. Thus does the truth become the taproot of our spiritual growth. Only the truth can bring our spiritual account into balance. When we operate in the channel of truth we access the power of God and we are living in His economy. In exchange for the pain truth brings to our life, we are rewarded with sanity, where we can see and act on the truth about alcohol. Peace and comfort comes to us, and our life becomes one of promise and purpose"

God as we misunderstand Him is our starting point

Oldtimer said, "We alcoholics tend to project our ideas onto God. These ideas are full of our own shortcomings, defects and faults which result in a misunderstanding and distorted perception of God as vengeful, unloving and controlling. When we do our inventory, we find that many of the faulty characteristics we attributed to the God of our understanding, we had them as well.

The old adage, "If you can spot it, then you got it" also applies to our relationship with God. This is why we encourage newcomers to have an open mind towards all spiritual matters, and consider the possibility of a loving, kind, merciful, forgiving God. Our understanding of God changes as we experience the unconditional love and unconditional acceptance we find in Alcoholics Anonymous. We feared we would be rejected if people knew exactly who we were. Yet, in the fellowship, we are loved by our fellow alcoholics, who know us intimately because they arrived to the fellowship in the same condition. They, too, were riddled with the guilt, shame, regret, and remorse that bedevils every alcoholic who graces the doors of AA. They, too, had committed heinous, unforgivable acts, and had become a weak and pathetic creature worthy only of scorn and loathing from society. Yet they stood as powerful evidence of a loving and merciful God who loved them through their worst because, in His Infinite Knowledge, He knew they had done the best they could against the unstoppable juggernaut that is alcoholism. Yet they found His favor and grace in the Twelve Steps—a way of life that delivered them from the gates of insanity and death to a heavenly existence in the World of the Spirit. And it is through this new understanding that we, ourselves, come to accept the possibility that we have been wrong, not only about alcohol but about God as well.

When we develop a new relationship with our Creator we undergo a spiritual experience. This experience transforms us, and as we begin to undergo a personality change, we find that our ideas about God change as well. As we become kind, loving, merciful, and forgiving, the God of our understanding reflects such changes in His character. The old perception of God that someone planted in our mind when we were young withers away, and a new understanding blossoms in our life as we experience His unwavering love.

With understanding comes acceptance, and our willingness to accept His will as our own increases as the miraculous begins to manifest in our life. In this new relationship with our Creator, His power flows into us and the obsession for alcohol is expelled from our mind. We find that we can recover from our hopeless state of mind and body, and live life successfully under any conditions."

Resentment and the two by four rule

Oldtimer said, "Resentment is the number one manifestation of self that destroys alcoholics on a daily basis. If not dealt with properly, it never fails to derail our recovery.

Sober or drinking, we are dominated by the transgressions of other people. Some of these transgressions are real. Some are imagined. Both have the power to destroy our lives. When resentments dominate, us our ability to think clearly diminishes. False Evidence Appearing Real intensifies our resentment and the fear of losing something we have, or not getting something we want, pushes us further down the road to ruin.

Resentment crowds out all other thoughts from our mind until only our viewpoint remains. At this point, our vengeance is justified, we strike out at our transgressors, and the cycle of destruction continues between the warring parties. We are sure all would be right if the opposition would only subject themselves to our whims. Rarely does this happen. And if it does happen, we simply make more demands upon the opposing party until the conflict arises again.

If we are to live long and happily in this world, we must break this destructive cycle and master our resentments. We cannot wish away this spiritual malady that blocks us from God's Power. Resentment is a power that feeds our restless spirit and brings great destruction into our lives.

Our relief from this deadly manifestation of self lies in our kit of spiritual tools. We look upon our transgressors as sick people, and offer them the same love and tolerance we would cheerfully grant a sick friend. We know much of spiritual illness, for we have recognized it in ourselves. We offer them, and ourselves, to God to do with as He will, and seek freedom from the bondage of self that holds us prisoner to vengeance. When we seek vengeance, we swallow the poison and hope the other person will die. This is the insanity of resentment that only becomes apparent once we commit to living life on a spiritual basis. So we pray: "This is a sick person. How can I be helpful to them. God save me from being angry. Thy will be done."

Through this simple prayer, we rise above our human instincts and assume the mantle of service and forgiveness that brings us through the storm and delivers us to salvation in the realm of God's peace. When we ask, we receive the serenity we desire, the courage to change our perspective, and the wisdom that allows us to avoid the deadly trap of resentment. We are then in much less danger of fear, anger, excitement, worry, and self-pity.

In our freedom from bondage to self, we fit ourselves as agents for God and stand ready to meet our commitment to serve God and the people about us."

Giving thanks for our newfound Friend

Oldtimer said, "When we complete our Fifth Step, our fear of God leaves us and we feel His presence in our life. This spiritual experience is an extension of our Third Step decision to turn our will and life over to the care of God. We did so with trepidation, for as alcoholics we have committed offenses against the laws of man, nature and God. But we find that only after we take a short journey on the spiritual path, we begin to have a spiritual experience that redefines our understanding of God and our relationships with Him. We are no longer working with an idea about God, now we have entered a deeply personal relationship with our Creator.

When we started our spiritual quest, we knew of God through our fellow AA's experience. They shared their experience, strength, and hope which stemmed from their relationship with God. When we decided we wanted what they had, and became willing to go to any lengths to get it, we offered ourselves to God through a transformative prayer in the Third Step. We placed our faith in the experience of our fellow alcoholics, and began our pursuit of our own relationship with God by focusing on that within our thinking that kept us blocked off from him. We shared these shortcomings with another, and the resulting humility opened our hearts for God to enter into our lives in a way that is indeed miraculous. We no longer acted on faith, for God had become a certainty in our lives. The Great Reality had become a great fact in our life, so we thanked God in prayer, from the bottom of our hearts, that we know Him better. We suddenly realized that He has, and always will be, a part of our make-up, just as much as the feeling we have for a friend.

That feeling is love, and it is through love by which we connect to our newfound Friend.

Cultivating recovery by nurturing the God idea

Oldtimer said, "Deep down inside every man, woman, and child is the fundamental idea of God. Recovery is expanding this idea by uncovering and discarding the elements of our character that diminishes God's presence in our consciousness. It is this fundamental idea of God that is the spark that ignites a chain reaction that transforms our minds, burns away the obsession and sets us on course as an agents for God's will.

To see the miracle of God's work we must surrender to God's will. He provides what we need so long as we stay close to Him and perform His work well. Step Six is a willingness to discard the ideas, emotions, and attitudes that prevent us from experiencing God's Power and performing His work. This Power emanates from the fundamental idea of God within each of us. When we walk in faith, and live God's way of life, we remove the defects of character within us that block the power we need from entering our consciousness.

When we fully apply spiritual principles to our lives, we can look back in wonder at the evidence of God's abundant love, grace and mercy which was in our lives even before we entered the rooms of recovery. It is our life that becomes His work when we surrender to His will. Not only is the obsession for alcohol lifted from our mind, but we begin to rebuild a life we trashed by living life based on self-will. We gain true vision into our past, and realize that our safe arrival into AA was a blessing in disguise. Deluded by an alcoholic mind, we failed to realize that it was His love and mercy that protected us in our drinking days. Thankfully, we did not get what we deserved. That would be a plot six feet under. Instead, we received a reprieve from a fatal illness that kills one-hundred percent of those afflicted with it.

It is only when we cease fighting, and surrender to the Steps, that we are blessed with a new pair of glasses that brings into focus the wonder and glory of God's work in our life. As we continue to trudge the road to our happy destiny, we finally see that God had been doing for us what we could not do for ourselves long before we became aware of it. We once were the lost, but now we are found. We once were the blind, but now we see the radiance of God's Love that highlights every step we take on the path to recovery."

The chains of our defects of character bind us to alcohol

Oldtimer said, "The chains of alcoholism embrace us so gently that by time we became aware of them, they were too strong to break. We consumed alcohol until it finally consumed us.

There is an ancient Chinese proverb that describes this phenomenon perfectly: "The man takes the drink. The drink takes the man. The drink takes the drink."

Alcohol rules the alcoholic, mind, body and soul. It corrupted us from the inside out, leading us to violate our moral and philosophical convictions, and destroy everything we loved and held dear. It placed us beyond human aid, where no human power could break the chains of bondage alcohol gently wove around us one drink at a time. We are so far gone that we only find salvation through the Twelve Steps, where we find the mercy and grace of a loving God who restores us to sanity and empowers us to live up to our moral and philosophical convictions.

God does not strike us sane, whole, and pure without our assistance. We must let go of the links in the chain of bondage that we have relied upon to help us survive our alcoholic life. So we let go and let God. Faith without works is dead, and we must be active participants in this restoration process.

Through inventory, we identify the corruption alcohol has imposed upon our will. Our character assets have been twisted into character defects by the dis-ease we have with God. In Step Six, we become willing to have God remove the defective character traits. And in Step Seven, we accept God's divine timing in this transformation process. In some instances, the defect is removed. But in other instances, we are left with the defect and must trust His timing.

Our struggle with our shortcomings solidifies our dependence upon God as we become aware of the limits of our finite, human resources. As we continue to live His way of life, and clear the path for His power to flow into our life, we find that we are easily able to live up to our moral and philosophical convictions. Thus do we emerge from the darkness of our shame, and are reborn into the Sunlight of the Spirit."

Alcohol transforms us into weapons of mass destruction

Oldtimer said, "Alcoholics are weapons of mass destruction on the installment plan. We brought about mass destruction one life at a time, and it will take a lifetime of amends to repair the damage we wrought. We leave broken hearts and broken relationships in our wake. We spread discord and dysfunction wherever we go, because we place the gratification of our instincts for sex, society and security before the comfort, welfare, and well being of others.

In recovery, we seek to change the impact we have upon the lives of others by placing the principles of the program before our personal wants, motives, demands, and desires. We are hard on ourselves and considerate of others because our ability to bring harm to them is wired into our subconscious. We want what we want when we want it how we want it. This self-seeking attitude allows us to continue to harm others, and prevents the healing grace of God from entering our lives.

We try to play God in our life and the lives of others, with disastrous results. This often brings about resentment toward the object of our control, and sometimes against God Himself. When selfishness manifests in our life, it stems from the subconscious fear of scarcity. We deem God's grace insufficient, and believe that we will not get what we want, or we will lose what we have. To overcome this unnatural, inbred, self-centered fear, we must consciously cultivate a spirit of unconditional giving. We must learn to give of ourselves and expect nothing in return. This is the role that service plays in recovery.

"Meeting makers make it" is not a statement on meeting attendance, but a statement of service. Those who give of their time, energy, and efforts to make meetings happen are the meeting makers. Their unselfish concern for the welfare of their fellow alcoholics has begun to remedy the fatal selfishness that is inherent to the alcoholic mind.

We fit ourselves to be of maximum service to God and the people about us by helping the fellowship to function. Eventually, this selfless practice makes its way into our subconscious mind and allows for the spirit of giving to guide us in repairing the harm we brought into the lives of others. Thus do we become living examples of God's love, power and way of life, and begin to repair the wreckage of the past that accumulated out of our efforts to live life based on self-will.

Living in the spirit of amends is an amends to ourselves

Oldtimer said, "The spiritual life is not a theory. We must live it. In Steps Six and Seven, we adopt attitudes essential to the work that sets us in Steps Eight and Nine. Before we make amends to others, we amend the nature of our character by changing the nature of our relationship with God. It is this change that impacts the nature of our relationship with others. We have to live our amends by adhering to the spiritual principles of the Steps. Only by doing so can the alcoholic avoid a return to the ravages of alcoholism, and revisit the harms we inflicted upon others.

Our amends must be a constant attitude, not an occasional act. The one person we owe a definite amends to is ourselves. Some look at this at selfish, but it is really a case of enlightened selflessness. Our amends to ourselves is not self-seeking in nature, nor is it born out of the alcoholic desire to seek our comfort above everything else. The amends we make to ourselves requires us to do what we do not want to do, and to find comfort in feeling uncomfortable.

Change is the essence of recovery, and amends means change. This can only happen when we make a decision of the heart to go to any lengths for sobriety. Once we sincerely make the Third Step decision, all sorts of remarkable things follow. So long as we remain willing to accept the things we cannot change, and summon the courage to change the things within ourselves that we can, we begin making amends to ourselves.

In making this decision, we change our fundamental approach to life. We are hard on ourselves and considerate of others. We make amends to ourselves by making amends to others. We make amends to ourselves by continuing to watch for the agents of alcoholism: selfishness, dishonesty, resentment, and fear. When these agents invade our thinking, we ask God to serve them an eviction notice. We no longer allow others to live rent-free in our minds. So we put out of our minds the wrongs they had done us, and turn our thoughts to others we can help.

Service is the secret ingredient for amending our lives. For in giving of ourselves to help others we receive God's grace, and His grace always heals the channel through which it flows. We make amends to ourselves by employing prayer and meditation in our daily life, asking not for ourselves, but for others we may help. It is in giving to others we that receive from God. So long as we maintain our focus on God's will for us, rather than our own will, we are blessed with a new attitude and new outlook on life which brings us a sense of joy and serenity we had never experienced.

Through our amends we are reborn into the World of the Spirit"

When in doubt Step Ten is the next right thing

Oldtimer said, "Do the next right thing" is an AA concept that has been taken out of context. It is not a loop hole that gives us free reign to harm others, and allows us to continue to act out on old behavior, just because we're human. Doing the next right thing relates to Step Ten. We acknowledge that we are indeed human and prone to making mistakes.

In Step Four we identified our four basic character defects that fueled our obsession for alcohol. Like the four basic colors from which we create a multitude of shades and hues, we use our selfishness, dishonesty, resentment, and fear in a multitude of ways to create the chaos and confusion that makes our lives unmanageable, and destroys our serenity.

The comfort that we once sought in the bottle has been replaced with terror, bewilderment, frustration and despair. Therefore, we continue to watch for selfishness, dishonesty, resentment, and fear as we go through each day. When these crop up in any form, the next right thing is to promptly ask God to remove the offending defect of character. The next right thing after that is to talk to some one about the situation. Usually, a closed mouth, understanding friend.

Our next right thing then becomes searching for, and making amends for any harm we may have committed in the past against anyone with our offensive behavior. And finally, the next right thing is to take the focus off of our selfish wants, motives, demands and desires, and turn our thoughts to someone we can help.

When we consistently apply the next right thing, our teachable Spirit creates a well of wisdom from which we draw the power to do the right thing. We are then able to rise above the shortcomings that block the road to our happy destiny. It turns our most devastating mistakes into valuable lessons that we use to assist others in their quest to live the AA way of life. In this way do we fail our way to success."

An alcoholic without prayer doesn't have a prayer

Oldtimer said, "We shouldn't be shy on this matter of prayer. Better men than we are using it constantly. It works, if we have the proper attitude and work at it."

Alcoholics have long used prayer as another self-seeking tool. Our prayer life, if we practiced at all, was focused on our physical comfort. Never did we pray for spiritual development. When we came to AA seeking help, we found that underlying our hopeless state of mind and body was a spiritual malady that prevented us from receiving the power we needed to recover.

Lack of power was truly our dilemma. We were physically powerless over alcohol due to a craving for alcohol that dominated us. Once we take the first drink, we cannot control our consumption of alcohol. Over time, our consumption of alcohol increased to devastating levels, and the consequences were just as devastating. If this were our only problem, we wouldn't have a need for prayer. We could use self-will, self-knowledge, reason, logic, and common sense to stop drinking. But the problem of the alcoholic centers in the mind, and an obsession for that which is destroying our lives.

Self-centered thinking denies us access to the power we need to overcome our obsession of the mind. God can and will relieve us of our obsession for alcohol, if we earnestly seek Him and follow the **G**ood **O**rderly **D**irections provided us in the Steps. When we do so, we are introduced to selfless prayer. We have a fatal selfishness that threatens us with a return to the bottle if not properly addressed. This selfishness permeates our thoughts, emotions and attitude. This is the essence of alcoholic ego that blocks God's power from our lives and dooms us to a downward spiral to the gates of insanity and death.

God has the power we need to transform our mind and relieve us of our insane desire for drink. The ego blocks God from our consciousness and reigns supreme in our mind. It will not rid itself of the old ideas, emotions and attitudes that allows it to dominate our life. By following and sustaining a course of action designed to reduce our ego, we allow for the flow of God's power into our lives so that we can grow spiritually and create a life greater than any we ever imagined. This is the focus of our prayer life. We pray for release from the bondage to the ego, and act in service to God and our fellow man.

Prayer and service are the key to our freedom from alcohol. We pray for release from our resentments, and ask how we can serve those who anger us. We pray for release from fear and ask how we can serve God. These prayers demonstrate the selflessness we need to escape a free fall into the first drink. It is the proper use of prayer for the self-centered alcoholic"

God's power flows through us to the sick and suffering alcoholic

Oldtimer said, "The Twelve Steps are a power move designed to remove the barriers between us and God, that we might gain access to His Infinite Power. We are powerless over alcohol, and suffer from a hopeless state of mind and body that places us beyond human aid. Frothy emotional appeal from our loved ones fail to provide the necessary impetus to drive us away from the drink. The warning of a doctor of an impending health crisis caused by our drinking proves an insufficient force in our battle against the bottle. With the alcoholic, there is a complete failure of the survival instinct that has aided human existence from the dawn of man's existence.

Only a spiritual awakening creates a connection to the God, and brings His power into our lives. And it is this power that transforms our thoughts, feelings and perception. This power heals the shame that binds us to the wreckage of our past, and sets our feet upon the road to a happy destiny. Once we have established this connection, we have to keep it clear by following the disciplines of Steps Ten, Eleven and Twelve.

There are many distractions on our path to redemption. So we must be ever-vigilant in avoiding the ego traps that offer us pleasure, but often result in shame. We continue to watch for selfishness, dishonesty, resentment and fear. When these crop up, we ask God to remove them at once. We talk to someone immediately about it, and make amends quickly if we have harmed anyone. Doing so empowers us to do the right thing in the face of old temptations.

In Step Eleven, we seek knowledge of God's will for us and the power to carry it out. We then do the next right thing and pray for the power to do the right thing. If we sense a loss of His power in our life, it is probably because we are going places God doesn't want us to go, seeing people God doesn't want us to see, and doing things God does not want us to do. There will be great interruptions to our pleasures in our walk with God, but we grow through them when we stay focused on Step Twelve. We continue to practice these power principles in all of our affairs, and continue to carry the message to the sick and suffering alcoholic. This creates a channel for His grace to flow. A grace that heals the one who transmits it, as well as the one who receives it.

When two are gathered in His name, doing His work, God's Power flows and provides what we need. In doing His work, we sense the nearness of His Spirit flowing in and through us. Thus do we become His agents. Empowered to help other alcoholics to recover."

Sobriety on self-will is a prelude to a relapse

Oldtimer said, "If we are able to stay sober on self-will alone then we are free to live life our terms. Unfortunately, life on our terms results in stinking thinking which soon evolves into stinking drinking.

The problem of the alcoholic centers in the mind. Not just in our conscious mind, but in our subconscious mind as well. We may command dominion over our conscious mind, but our subconscious mind consistently commands dominion over our conscious mind. And it is the existence of our obsession for alcohol in our subconscious mind that makes alcohol cunning, baffling and powerful to us. Therefore, our ability to stay sober by force of will alone proves insufficient. We cannot provide an effective mental defense against the first drink because we do not have command and control over our entire mind. We are powerless over our subconscious thoughts, and our alcoholic mind routinely entertains thoughts that reinforce the notion that alcohol does something for us when in reality alcohol was doing something very bad to us.

This is the insanity of our alcoholic mind. We are at, certain times, unable to see and act on the truth about alcohol. It is a poisonous form of pleasure that consumes us even as we consume it. The truth sets us free from the ravages of our alcoholic mind, but we must rigorously pursue it if we are to find freedom from our bondage to delusion. Only through an entire psychic change do we prepare our mind to cultivate the truth. As we release that which is false, our thought life rises to a higher plane nearer to God. We feel the nearness of His presence, and in this spiritual experience we are restored to the truth. And as we continue to pursue the truth, dominion over our mind is given to God.

Every day we pursue the vision of His will by practicing the principles of AA in all of our affairs. Thus do we continue to grow in His image and in the truth we find a fourth dimension of existence that gets infinitely more wonderful as time passes."

The battle of the bottle is won when we let God fight it

Oldtimer said. "The insanity of the first drink is the front line in recovery. However, we do not fight this battle alone. We cannot see and act on the truth about our relationship with alcohol. We have lost the power of choice over the drink. No matter how intelligent we maybe in other matters, we are strangely insane when it comes to alcohol. We lack an effective mental defense against the first drink. And once we take the first drink, we lose control over how much we will drink.

We have an abundance of experience that demonstrates our inability to control our consumption of alcohol, yet we repeatedly try the desperate experiment of the first drink. If we are to recover, we have to smash the idea that somehow, someday we will control and enjoy our drinking. We cannot win this battle of wits with alcohol. It has a firm grasp on our thought system, so we surrender to God and let Him fight the battle for us.

It is a battle we have always lost, and will always lose. But it is a battle God has never lost, and cannot lose, so long as we allow Him to fight it without our interference!

This is the ultimate act of love He provides for the sick and suffering alcoholic. He will provide what we need, so long as we stay close to Him and do His work (the Steps) well. This is our part in the battle. We focus our time, energy and effort on growing and expanding our spiritual life. By doing so, we expand our consciousness and bring the Power of God to bear on our alcohol problem. Over time, we learn that His Power is not limited to our drinking problem, but is available to us in all of our affairs. We need only let go of our insistence on running the show ourselves, and let God's power affect a change in our life. When we do so we are pleased with the results, and become much more willing to accept His will in all of our affairs. Thus do we become agents for God, demonstrating His omnipotence as we overcome our human problems with grace and glory, while carrying our story of redemption to the sick and suffering alcoholic."

Surrender brings the joy of freedom from a fatal malady

Oldtimer said, "Surrender means we completely give ourselves to the AA program, in the same way we surrendered our will and life to alcohol. We let nothing come between us and our desire for a drink. We were willing to sink to any depth of depravity to live life on alcohol's terms. Therefore, we must have the same commitment to recovery. We must be willing to go to any lengths to live life on God's terms, that we might recover from a hopeless state of mind and body.

Half-measures avail us nothing. Neither does a ninety-nine percent effort. We must give one-hundred percent effort one-hundred percent of the time if our surrender is to be effective. Whatever we place in front of recovery will be the first thing we lose when we relapse. There cannot be any lurking notions about the futility and fatality of our condition. We have an illness that centers in our mind. Even with this knowledge, and many examples of failures that may have preceded them, some alcoholics continue to trust their faulty thinking and try to recover on their own terms.

They only comply, rather than surrender. They stop drinking and only alter their life to the extent they find comfortable, with a reservation that at some point they will be able to safely return to drinking.

This is often a fatal delusion. Alcoholics cannot safely imbibe in alcohol or any other intoxicant. Be it liquid, leaf, pill, or powder, our attempts at chemical peace of mind only drive us deeper into the pits of pitiful and incomprehensible demoralization. We must be willing to go to any lengths if we expect to escape the final, fatal consequences of alcoholism and live long and happily in this world.

We may not know what life holds for us in recovery, what we will have to do to stay sober, or where we will have to go, so we must be willing trust God and practice the principles of recovery in all of our affairs. When we do so we live life happy, joyous, and free with faith that God's will won't lead us where his grace cannot protect us."

Our fears fall from us and we experience the presence of our Creator

Oldtimer said, "Alcoholics are driven by fear. Many of these fears are unknown to us, and only by applying inventory to our lives on a daily basis are we able to bring into our consciousness the impact fear has on our lives.

We fear what others think of us, and this results in pride. We fear we will be physically or emotionally harmed and this results in anger. We fear there isn't enough material sustenance to meet our needs, and this results in greed and gluttony. We fear our lives are inadequate, so we covet and envy that which others possess. Our fear of inadequacy extends to our sex life where we believe we don't have enough sex, or it isn't the right flavor, and this results in lust. We fear success, and at the same time we fear failure, and this paralysis by analysis leads to sloth.

Fear bedeviled every facet of our life. We must develop a deep abiding faith that will overcome our debilitating fear. As tactile people, alcoholics only believe what they experience. This is why fear dominates our belief system. Every fear is based on an experience we had in the past. This is why we are encouraged to live just for today. But we cannot do this unless we have a spiritual experience that brings us into direct conscious contact with God. This spiritual experience is more than sufficient to overcome our fear-based belief system, for all doubt of God's existence will be obliterated by the release of His power into our life. When we lose our fear we experience His presence in our life. And this experience further obliterates the fear that distorts our perception and makes our life unmanageable.

Once we make conscious contact with our Creator, we no longer need liquid courage, nor do we need to have faith in the unseen. For our eyes have seen the coming of the glory of God with every sober breath we take. He has entered our lives and commenced to do for us what we could not do for ourselves—expel the fears that prevented us from living long and happily in this world."

Walking in the humility of the truth sets us free

Oldtimer said, "When a person is humiliated it has a major impact on them. Humiliation is when humility is forced upon you. We experience this in our First Step experience. We had to admit we were wrong about our relationship with alcohol. This broke our pride and brought us to our bottom. We reached a point where we had come to believe in the hopelessness and futility of life as we had been living it. We later found that when we were down to our bottom God was up to something. It is only when we hit bottom that we are prepared to look at life from an entirely different angle and take the actions necessary to develop the vision required to bring God into our lives. When we go forward on faith our vision becomes clearer.

In the Fourth Step, we clear away the wreckage that has clouded our vision. In Step Five we begin to experience the miraculous. Humility carries with it the quiet power of truth. And it is the truth we share that sets us free from our deadly pride and fatal self-centeredness. We now have a new pair of glasses that bring the vision of God into our reality.

Fifth Step Promises

"We pocket our pride and go to it, illuminating every twist of character, every dark cranny of the past. Once we have taken this step, withholding nothing, we are delighted. We can look the world in the eye. We can be alone at perfect peace and ease. Our fears fall from us. We begin to feel the nearness of our Creator. We may have had certain spiritual beliefs, but now we begin to have a spiritual experience. The feeling that the drink problem has disappeared will often come strongly. We feel we are on the Broad Highway, walking hand in hand with the Spirit of the Universe."

Thus do we begin our walk with God in earnest. He does not make too hard terms with those who earnestly seek Him, and our earnestness has brought us into a deeper conscious contact with Divine Intelligence. Be we atheist, agnostic, or any of the numerous religions, the Highway to Heaven is broad with room for all to enter.

This experience is the beginning of the end for our alcoholic thinking. The spiritual experience brings us acceptance, humility and forgiveness, and the shame, guilt, regret, and remorse that robbed us of our peace of mind is now gone. Peace and serenity now comes to us naturally. Rather than seeking escape from reality through the drink, we seek the Great Reality within by sharing the truth of our existence with God and another person.

Once we have done this we are truly on the path to recovery. And if God has one hand, and a newcomer has the other, it becomes impossible for us to pick up a drink."

No pain no change. No change no gain

Oldtimer said, "In developing a new relationship with our Creator, we must also develop a new attitude with ourselves that allows God to manage our affairs from the inside out.

Step Six requires a change in our perspective and outlook toward pain, as well as our relationship with God, ourselves, and the people about us. In Step Six, we adopt an attitude of willingness. Faith means courage, and it takes courage to change.

Forever **A**lways **I T**rust **H**im who has all power and is our salvation. God is Infinite Power, Infinite Knowledge, and Infinite Love. And He is willing to bless us with what we need when we need it and how we need it. We must be willing to prepare ourselves to receive His blessings. We must empty ourselves and let go of the old ideas, emotions and attitudes that enabled and supported our drinking. No more **E**asing **G**od **O**ut. The more we empty ourselves of ego, the more room there is for God in our lives.

Often God's blessings come to us in the form of a lesson that shows us what it is we must let go. With our new attitude, we find our blessings in that which disturbs us. For years we sought our comfort in alcohol. This self-seeking behavior does not change overnight. It can take a lifetime. Right feelings follow right actions, but not right away. So we must condition ourselves to feel comfortable with feeling uncomfortable.

We seek progress in Step Six, not perfection. We find that when we are disturbed we have the problem. So we ask God to take away the difficulty within ourselves that is the true source of our troubles, and we prepare ourselves to walk through the pain of accepting that which is unacceptable to our ego—God's will.

This new attitude of willingness allows us to continue to pursue the self-searching that levels our pride and allows us to continue to confess our shortcomings to those we have harmed. Step Six requires us to go beyond our comfort zone and walk through the pain that comes with change.

No pain, no change. No change, no gain.

We must be willing to embrace pain as the taproot of our spiritual growth. No true transformation can occur without pain, and it is through the pain of spiritual growth that we inherit a life more abundant.

Until the pain of remaining the same becomes greater than the pain of doing what is needed to initiate change in our life, alcoholics simply do not change. And if we do not change, we may well exchange our sobriety date for an expiration date. If we expect to live long and happily in this life, we must be willing to open our mind to the truth God reveals to us, no matter how much pain that truth bears. When we do so, we are blessed with His power and love. Such is the nature of His way of abundant life.

Steps Six and Seven are the economy of the Spiritual World

Oldtimer said, "When we live fully in the spirit of Steps Six and Seven, it can truly be said that we have been restored to our right standing with God. We know who we are and Whose we are. We live in the economy of the Spirit, where we give to receive. We have a new Employer that provides what we need, when we need it, and how we need it.

In this economy, God's grace is our currency. We unconditionally give the love we received in AA to the newcomer. In doing so, we are relieved of our deadly selfishness, and live a life more abundant in Spirit. And as we grow in Spirit, we are endowed with the gifts of our Creator that serve to increase our effectiveness and understanding of the world about us. No longer are we in full flight from reality, for we have found the Great Reality within and we have been restored to sanity as a result. No longer do we do the same thing over again and over again expecting a different result. Our Teachable Spirit has awakened and we prosper on the spiritual level with every failure we encounter on the material level. No weapon formed against us shall prosper, so long as we continue to reside in the World of the Spirit.

This is not a flight of fantasy, but a simple truth for those who earnestly seek to enlarge and grow their spiritual life. No one who seeks to find the truth can fail to find God in the midst of their pursuit. Once we awaken to the truth, we awaken to God. When we have a spiritual awakening we join a Fellowship of the Spirit that stretches back to the dawn of man.

Alcoholics are not the only ones who experience a spiritual awakening. This miraculous event has been occurring from the beginning of time. But no one has ever needed this experience more than the alcoholic. Without it we perish. So we humbly submit to God our will and life, and we live to the best of our ability the Twelve Steps of Recovery AA offers. In this way we are not only restored to sanity, but empowered by the Sunlight of the Spirit to grow in the image of our Creator and develop a life based on wisdom, love, and courage where we help others to cultivate their spiritual life. In doing so, we are blessed with more grace than we deserve. And so long as we walk the path of recovery, the best days of our lives will always lay before us."

Love is forgiving and forgiving others is loving ourselves

Oldtimer said, "Putting out of our minds the harm others have done us, we resolutely search for the harms we have done others. When we review our amends list, we need to consider not only those we owe amends, but those we need to forgive. Until we have truly forgiven those on our amends list who may have harmed us, we will not be able to place out of our minds the wrongs they have done to us. Our readiness to forgive determines whether we are entirely ready to make complete amends to them. Are we entirely ready to look at our dysfunctional relationships from a different angle?

We look upon those who harmed us as spiritually sick people who harmed us in an attempt to heal themselves. Spiritually sick people hurt other people because they have been hurt themselves. Very likely, we are the ones who made them sick, and just like us, they sought comfort by arranging life to suit themselves. With this is mind, we consider the 2 x 4 rule. Our transgressors intent was not 2 do something to us. They were doing something 4 themselves. Very often they harmed us out of self defense, or in response to a harm we visited upon them.

Keeping our side of the street clean means we offer forgiveness where it is warranted, and then prepare to make the necessary amends. At some of these we balk, and in that case, we list our amends according to those we are willing to forgive now, those we are willing to forgive later, those we may or may not be willing to forgive, and those we are never going to forgive. For these more difficult amends we need to pray for God's will for us in each matter, and ask for the willingness to be willing to forgive them. We will find that as we seek forgiveness for ourselves we prove worthy of the freedom and peace forgiveness brings. So those who we delay making amends to become beacons of true freedom, peace, and serenity. And once we make our peace of mind non-negotiable, the willingness to forgive the unforgivable becomes a top priority in our life. When this happens we can truly say that we are free to love, free to live and free to forgive. For we are living in the image of our Creator, who forgives us in the measure we offer forgiveness to others."

Out of self and into God

Oldtimer said, "Alcoholics Anonymous is a way of life centered not on self, but on service to God and others. Our recovery is not based on a superior intellect, nor is it based on a superior religious practice. It is based on a willingness to go to any lengths to change.

Amends means change, and the change we seek is brought about by following the path or recovery AA offers. Those AA members who are most successful are the ones who completely give themselves to the Twelve Steps. They gave up on their way of life and adopted God's way of life as their own. We consider this way of life when we come into the rooms, learn the fatal nature of our illness, and the spiritual solution AA offers. We then make a decision. We either choose to live life on a spiritual basis, or we roll the dice and rely on self-will to keep us sober. If we decide to live life on a spiritual basis, we learn to do so by applying Steps Four through Nine to our lives. The essence of these Steps is amends, or change.

In Step One, we amend the nature of our relationship with our drinking, and set the bottle down. In Step Two, we amend our relationship with our thinking. In Step Three, we amend our relationship with God. In Step Four and Five, we amend our relationship with the truth. In Steps Six and Seven, we amend our relationship with pain, and this brings us to the essential amends of Steps Eight and Nine which bring about a change in our relationship with others. We then continue to practice what we learned in this process, one day at a time.

In practicing the principles of the program in all of our affairs, to best of our ability, we make progress on the elimination of selfishness and the growth of selflessness. We get out of self, and into God. The less self we have in our being the more God we have in our being. And the more God we have in our being, the more room we have in our life for others.

Everyday is a day we must carry the vision of God's will into all of our activities. Everyday is a day when we fit ourselves to be of maximum service to God and the people about us. This requires the rigorous application of Steps Ten, Eleven, and Twelve in all of our affairs. On a daily basis, we learn to get out of self. Through the continuing use of inventor, we identify, and become willing to let go of, the character defects that stand in the way of our usefulness to God and our fellow man. We get deeper into God through consistent prayer and meditation. And we get into others by carrying the AA message to the sick and suffering alcoholic.

As we continue to practice this process, we become effective agents for God, dedicated to the advancement of His creation."

The battle against the bottle takes place in the mind

Oldtimer said, "The battle against the bottle is one an alcoholic must undertake on a daily basis. It is a battle we not only fight hard, but one in which we also fight smart.

The problem of the alcoholic centers in the mind, not the body, not the bottle, nor the barroom. We have an obsession of the mind that drives us to a delusional state where we believe a drink is a good idea, in spite of overwhelming evidence that proves beyond a shadow of doubt that drinking is a very bad idea.

To win this battle we must surrender to the AA program in order to win at life. To win any battle against an enemy it is crucial to cut the supply lines. We do the same in our battle against the bottle. At first glance it would appear we fight the battle against alcoholism by cutting off the supply line to the drink. We stop drinking and change playmates, playgrounds and playthings. Bu this is an insufficient change if we expect to win this battle for our life. We must surrender completely. First from the drink, then from self-will and then to God's will.

Putting down the bottle is the first battle we must fight. It takes great fortitude for an alcoholic to accomplish this task, but the ultimate battle is won internally by cutting off the supply line to our maniacal obsession for the drink. If we are successful at doing this, we will find a that lifetime of success awaits us.

The supply line we seek to cut is self-will. Selfishness, dishonesty, resentment, and fear are the manifestations of self that fuel the obsession, and it is these maladies that lay at the root of our unmanageable life. Without alcohol an alcoholic is left in a restless, irritable and discontented state. Our mind seeks relief from this state. When we can't drink, we try to arrange our external life to bring comfort to our internal state. But in doing so, we only create an external mess that reflects our inner disturbance. A disturbance that we once again seek to sooth with alcohol. We seek the chemical peace of mind that we used to find in the first drink. But it is a drink that now brings on an alcoholic spree which leaves us in a state of pitiful and incomprehensible demoralization.

When we make a commitment to our natural peace of mind, we go beyond what is convenient, and do whatever is necessary for us to attain and maintain our serenity. Each day we continue to watch for the disturbing defects of character that seem to rule our mind, and leave us restless, irritable and discontented. We ask God to remove these defects so that we may grow beyond our alcoholic limitations and maintain our inner peace. By doing so, we starve the mental obsession of the energy it needs to drive us back to the bottle.

As we set aside our right to manage our affairs, and follow the dictates of a Higher Power, our lives become manageable, and we no longer pursue the chemical peace of mind we once sought in the bottle. In this newfound freedom we find joy, happiness, and a life more abundant. The more frequently we abide in God's will, the further we move from the bottle, and our victory over alcohol is assured as we trudge the road to our happy destiny in a fourth dimension of existence that gets infinitely more wonderful as time passes."

Prayer paves the way for God to enter our mind

Oldtimer said, "The alcoholic lacks an effective mental defense against the first drink. And for the alcoholic, to drink is to die.

Our defense must come from a deep, abiding relationship with a Higher Power. In this relationship, we must effectively communicate with God through prayer and meditation. For the alcoholic to develop an effective prayer life, we must constantly employ inventory. An effective prayer is one that implores God to remove the manifestations of self that prevents us from seeking his will. This is selfless prayer that fits us for maximum service to God and the people about us. Selfish prayer would have God follow our will. Such self-seeking only strengthens our defects of character. And it is these shortcomings that lead us down the path of relapse.

If we expect to live long and happily in this world, we must continue to watch for selfishness, dishonesty, resentment, and fear. When these crop up, we humble ourselves and pray for God to remove them. Thus do we find serenity and transform our character defects into character assets. When we live the AA way of life, it is our shortcomings that become the inspiration for our prayer life. These defects will reveal themselves many times each day, so we pause when agitated and doubtful, and ask God for the right thought or action. The answer will come if we want it.

Taking proper inventory requires us to apply rigorous honesty in pursuit of our wrongs. We learn that our mind is the battlefield, and is often our worst enemy. One lesson we learn from inventory is the fallibility of the mind. We cannot place one-hundred percent faith in a mind that has been corrupted by years of drinking and delusional thinking. If we are to grow in the image of our Creator, we must humbly admit our wrongs and shortcomings on a daily basis.

Pride and fear are the double-edged sword of delusion that will retard our spiritual progress if we do not learn overcome them. Pride tells us we need not look at our flaws, for they do not exist. Fear tells us we dare not look at our flaws, for they will destroy us. So we learn to live in a state of active prayer. We start with prayer in the morning, and upon awakening ask God to reveal His will to us, and grant us the power to carry it out. We end our day with prayer before we retire for the night. We thank God for our daily bread, sobriety. By doing so, we develop the willingness to humbly submit throughout the day to God's will, and pray many times "Thy will, not mine, be done." We are then safe and protected from an obsession of the mind that seeks to restore us to drunkenness and, thus, insure our destruction."

Helping the sick and suffering alcoholic keeps us sober

Oldtimer said, "If God is holding one of our hands and the newcomer is holding on to the other, it is impossible for us to pickup a drink. This analogy projects the image of security for the alcoholic in AA. So long as we are living in the selfless principles of the AA program we are safe and protected from relapse.

Some alcoholics choose to gamble on the meetings. They believe, and have been told, that attending meetings is insurance against picking up the first drink. This was never the AA solution to alcoholism. In fact, it is the epitome of the alcoholic seeking their comfort and taking the easier, softer road.

AA founder Dr. Bob attended Oxford Group meetings religiously. He also drank religiously while attending those meetings. It wasn't until Bill Wilson added the secret ingredient of working with other alcoholics to what Dr. Bob had learned in the Oxford Group, that he was able to escape the alcoholic pit. He spent the next fifteen years working with drunks in order to insure his sobriety.

Even today, millions of alcoholics drink after attending an AA meeting. But the delusional alcoholic, who fears both God and alcohol, pretends to recover by making a geographical change from the bar room to the rooms of recovery. They fail to understand the fatal nature of our shared malady, and choose to work a program that has been repeatedly proven to fail.

The problem of the alcoholic is centered in the mind. Over time, perhaps over a significant period of time, the drink idea takes over the mind and the alcoholic makes a geographic change back to the bar room. At the root of the alcoholic's problem is selfishness and self-centeredness. This is our comfort zone. We must lose this selfishness or die. And only through the altruistic action of helping others are we able to escape the debilitating pull of our self-centeredness.

Everyday is a day we carry the vision of God's will for us into our all of our activities. Everyday is a day we must give of ourselves to the sick and suffering alcoholic, so that we may live long and happily in this world. We give to live, and in doing so, others join us on the high road to happy destiny."

Alcohol is a power greater than ourselves that only God can overcome

Oldtimer said, "The disease of alcoholism is centered in the mind, and it requires an entire psychic change to overcome its destructive power. This means we must have an open mind toward all spiritual matters. For our disease is really a dis-ease with God. And since the solution to the disease of alcoholism is a spiritual experience, this creates a malady within us when we reject the only solution to our lack of power over alcohol.

Alcohol is a power greater than the alcoholic that transformed our ideas, emotions and attitudes, and disconnected us from our spiritual nature. It became a god unto us that commanded of us many self-destructive behaviors. If we are to be free of its influence, we must be willing to let go of all our old ideas about God and spiritual matters. After all, they didn't work for us. If they did, we wouldn't find ourselves in Alcoholics Anonymous. If we do not change the person we were when we first came into the rooms of recovery, that person will go back out for another drink. This is a guarantee of alcoholism. It has been proven by millions who failed to perfect and enlarge their spiritual life. We either change our lives to fit the Steps, or we will exchange our sobriety for inebriation.

If we are fortunate, we survive our relapse and make it back to the rooms of recovery. The fatal nature of alcoholism is an idea the alcoholic mind often rejects. In fact, it rebels against the thought of any life without alcohol, and is willing to bet our life on it. The old idea that alcohol is doing for us what we could not do for ourselves has to be smashed. At one time it did work for us. But those days are long gone. In fact, it is now working against us, and doing things to us that we would never do to ourselves. So degraded is our alcoholic life that any change is an improvement.

AA not only offers us a life preserver, but an opportunity to rebuild our lives on a solid foundation that will withstand the trials and tribulations that are sure to enter our life. We will no longer need to take a flight from reality on the wings of alcohol, but instead embrace every challenge life presents as an opportunity to demonstrate the power of God's omnipotence. He restores our sanity when we lose our faith in our limited human power, and place our faith in the unlimited power, love and wisdom we find in His way of life."

We find sanity in our primary purpose

Oldtimer said, "Our primary purpose is to stay sober and help others achieve sobriety. Our purpose drives our choices. Our choices drive our actions. Our actions bring about the consequences that constitute our life.

Alcoholics are often confused between their needs and wants. Recovery simplifies that choice. We have a fatal illness and our recovery from it is based on our willingness to live a spiritual life and help others. Therefore, we must choose between what we want and what we need. Our want cup is bottomless and can never be filled. Our need cup overflows with God's grace when we surrender to His way of life.

Often, recovery is doing what we don't want to do in order to get what we need. The ego wants for satisfaction of our impulses for sex, society, and security. Unfortunately, when we give in to these impulses, it only creates a deeper desire for more of the same. It could be said that these impulses are the natural cravings of the body. However, when we Ease God Out in order to satisfy our instincts, we fall from His grace and open ourselves up to the pitiful and incomprehensible demoralization of another relapse–a return to drinking which brings terror, bewilderment, frustration and despair into our lives once again.

When we make a decision to live up to our primary purpose, we choose to live each day on a spiritual basis and use our kit of spiritual tools in all of our affairs. By doing so, we fit ourselves for maximum service to others, who are in need of purpose and direction as they attempt to walk the path of recovery. When we stay close to God and perform His work well, he provides what we need to satisfy our instincts in a manner that will enhance our spiritual life. When we surrender to God's will, we find that His love protects us from the ravages of the alcohol, and provides us with a barrier to further self-destruction with freedom from the bondage of self and the dysfunctional habits we have acquired.

Ye though we walk through the valley of the shadow of death, we shall fear no evil, for our life is in the care of a loving, merciful God. When we live His way of life, we lose our fear of today, tomorrow, and the hereafter. And so long as we remain true to our primary purpose, and keep on the path of recovery, we will find a happy destiny awaiting us at the end of our days."

God's way of life brings the sanity we seek

Oldtimer said, "When we live God's way of life, we are restored to sanity in regard to our ability to see and act on the truth about our relationship with alcohol. Initially, we find release from the bondage to alcohol, but we must go much further to repair the damage it inflicted upon our personality.

When you take alcohol away from an alcoholic horse thief, you are still left with a horse thief. Our progress through the Steps demands a continuous change in our personality. If we cease drinking and maintain an alcoholic personality, some situation in life, either a failure or a success, will lead us back to the bottle. We must continue to enlarge and perfect our spiritual life so that we can overcome the pitfalls of life without the a return to drinking. We must put away our childish emotions, ideas, and attitudes, and grow along spiritual lines.

We achieve intellectual and emotional sobriety by aiming for spiritual perfection. For only when our aim is high do we achieve the necessary spiritual progress. Everyday is a day we must keep an open mind toward all spiritual matters. When we do so our Teachable Spirit will bring us human teachers to help us develop our spiritual life. We may not like these teachers. In fact, we may resent them, or even be fearful of them. But as long as we are willing to pick up the kit of spiritual tools we have acquired in the Steps, we will grow through even the most unpleasant situations. We will no longer run and hide from the source of our fears, but acknowledge that, though we may walk in the shadow of doubt, God is with us. His presence will order our steps. And in those situations where anger, hate, and resentment arise, we turn our thoughts to forgiveness, with the understanding that the party we resent is spiritually sick, just as we are, and that our only aim is to be helpful and to serve God's will in the affair.

Freedom from the bondage of self is not an overnight matter. It may take a lifetime. But we must undergo continual spiritual development so that our defective mental state is restored, and we can adjust to life by accepting reality on God's terms. In this way do we turn our bedevilments into blessings that allow us to become contributing members of a society we once scorned and brought destruction upon."

We inventory that which separates us from God

Oldtimer said, "To thine own self be true. Truth brings about awareness. Awareness brings about acceptance. Acceptance brings about action.

As we continue to apply prayer and meditation to our lives we begin to expose the levels of delusion we've built up over the years. This is why we must embrace rigorous honesty as a way of life. By doing so, we are able to effectively apply the tools of recovery to the problem areas of our lives, and uncover that which is not our true self, and bring to the light of truth that which is our true self.

God created us in His image of truth, and in our alcoholism we created a false self to replace the self we viewed as vulnerable, weak, and flawed. For had we been able to accept our emotions, thoughts, and attitudes as they were, we would not have attempted to alter them with a mood-altering substance. We were not at peace with the truth, and spent years at war with ourselves. Now, the truth will set us free from that battle if we surrender our vulnerabilities, flaws and weaknesses to the care of God.

The Twelve Steps are God's infirmary for the alcoholic. Willingness is the key that unlocks the door to the truth of our being. We were restless, irritable and discontented, and sought peace in the bottle. But that only led to pitiful, incomprehensible demoralization. Only in the truth do we find peace of mind and comfort with our natural being. God is the Truth. So we launch on a course of rigorous house cleaning to rid ourselves of the worthless ideas, emotions, and attitudes that manifest into selfishness, resentment, fear and dishonesty which blocks us off from God.

Only Truth can dispel these impulses from our mind, and when it does so, peace prevails. When we are at peace with ourselves, we find no need to alter our moods, but we simply accept them as the natural order of life on God's terms."

When we surrender we come out of hiding

Oldtimer said, "Part of the surrender process requires us to come out from hiding. In Step Five, we reveal the secrets we have been hiding from the world. And in doing so, we find that there have been secrets we have been hiding from ourselves. We open our vault of shame, and share what was once a secret treasure. But now, in our new life in recovery, we find it is the trash of the past that keeps us bound to shame. It is this evidence we have been holding onto that convinces us that we are worthless trash. And as long as we keep it hidden, it keeps hidden from us the true treasure of our spiritual nature. So we admit to God, ourselves and another human being the exact nature of our wrongs. We admit it to God for forgiveness, to ourselves for acceptance, and to others for humility.

The nature of all the wrongs we have committed lies in the roots of a defective character created when we **E**ased **G**od **O**ut of our lives and went on to live a life of self will run riot. There is no peace in a riot. Where God is not present peace is impossible. So it is necessary for the sick and suffering alcoholic to open the channel by which God can enter our heart, and prepare our mind to receive the peace He offers.

It takes courage to undertake the actions that will grant us the wisdom that allow us to harvest sweet fruit from our bitter past. By confessing our wrongs, we find a peace that is not of this world. When it overcomes us we begin to feel the presence of our Creator. God enters into our hearts in a manner that is indeed miraculous, and the light of purity enters into our thought life.

In the light of this truth, we see that we are not our character defects, but something much greater-that which God created! It is this something we had thrown away as if it were trash. Now, we seek to recover it from the trash heap, for we now know it is the true treasure of our divine origin. It is our true self!"

Humility transforms pain into power

Oldtimer said, "Pain is the taproot of our spiritual growth because we hold onto our old ideas, emotions, and attitudes so fiercely that by time we let them go, they have our claw marks all over them. When we begin our walk on the path of recovery, we have more faith in these ideas than we have in God, and it takes a great deal of pain before we let go and let God take us to better things.

In Step Six, we pray for the willingness to be willing to let God take from us the character defects that stand in the way of our usefulness to Him and our fellow man. This prayer of the heart takes time to reach our mind, and it requires a great deal of pain before the mind accepts the prayers of the heart. Until the pain of staying the same becomes greater than the pain of changing, we will not change.

It took a great deal of agony before we let go of alcohol. It takes just as much pain to let go of the old ideas, emotions, and attitudes that we marinated in alcohol. They constitute the Internal Spiritual Malady of alcoholism that keeps us in bondage to the alcoholic mind.

After much humiliation brought on by our alcoholic sprees, we humbly admitted in Step One that we were wrong about our relationship with alcohol. In Step Two, we humbly admitted that we were wrong about our relationship with our mind. In Step Three, we humbly admitted that we were wrong about our relationship with God. In Steps Four and Five, we humbly admitted that we were wrong about our relationship with other people. And in Step Six and Seven, we humbly admitted that we were wrong about the value of our old ideas, emotions, and attitudes.

Humiliation is when humility is forced upon us. When this happens, we are weakened. When we humbly accept the truth about ourself we are empowered. Humility provides us a power so great that no weapon formed against us will prosper. It transforms our pain into power. As we accept the truth about our shortcomings, faults, and defects, our Teachable Spirit arises in us and allows us to prosper from every negative situation in our life, both past and present. In this way, our past becomes our most valuable treasure, and the present becomes the foundation upon which we build a bright future rooted in God, and the truth of our existence as servants in His ever-advancing creation."

The three A's of AA: Awareness, Acceptance, Action

Oldtimer said, "Awareness! Acceptance! Action!" This our rallying cry in recovery.

When we became aware of the path of destruction our drinking had taken us down, we accepted the AA solution and applied the spiritual program of action to our life. We began a pursuit of that which is true within us, and discarded that which was false. When we are true to ourselves, we bring the Sunlight of the Spirit to bear on our human nature and with this awareness we come to accept every shortcoming and defect of character we hold. We do not seek to keep them hidden from view, but, instead, bring them to light so that we can grow from them.

These defects of character will provide us guidance on our path to spiritual perfection. For we no longer desire to live by their rule, but by God's providence. So we accept them, and in prayer we ask God to remove the defects of character that stand in the way of our usefulness to Him and our fellow man. These shortcomings become the cornerstone of our prayer life which is directed towards selflessness and service. We ask for freedom from the bondage of self, that we may better do God's will, and we stand ready to let go of our flaws and let God use them for His Divine Purpose.

Although we may not be entirely willing to let go of these flaws in our make up, we ask God for the willingness to be willing. In doing so, we open ourselves up to a new relationship with pain. For it was through pain that we became willing to let go of the bottle and bring an end to the way of death we had been living. Now, it is through pain that we develop the willingness to let go of the defects of character that leave us short of God's perfect plan.

When the pain of staying the same becomes greater than the pain of change we are prepared to let go and let God. This is the unfortunate circumstance of the alcoholic. Only when pain replaced the pleasure we experienced with alcohol did we find the willingness to separate ourselves from drink for good. So it is with our defects. We must experience the pain of the circumstances presented by our shortcomings before we are ready to let God take us to a higher level of consciousness.

Eventually, we become driven by the pain of separation from God, and cease acting on our defects of character. He grants us the power to live up to our moral and philosophical convictions, rather than living down to base human instincts from which our defects are derived. When we no longer empower them they lose their grasp on our mind, and God's purpose and promise begins to dominate our thought life. Thus do we bring the ego to it's right size, and become the effective agents for God, empowered to work the miraculous in the lives of others."

Amends restore emotional balance

Oldtimer said, "If we continue to harm others, we are quite sure to drink. As alcoholics, we are punished by our sins in the here and now, not for them in the hereafter. Our feelings carry a fierce intensity. We don't love; we obsess. We don't hate; we resent. We don't fear; we are neurotic. We don't merely feel guilt when we've done wrong; we transform our guilty feelings into toxic shame. We internalize our guilt and judge ourselves by what we have done. Therefore, we have not done something bad, we are something bad!

In this state of shame, we judge ourselves unworthy of recovery, and accept the death sentence the bottle carries. This is why making amends is essential for our emotional sobriety. It relieves us of our alcoholic thinking and restores us to emotional balance when we admit our wrongs and make restitution for the harm we have caused.

This is difficult. For the alcoholic mind employs a scale of justice that places far more blame on our victims, and rationalizes our complicity in the dysfunctional relationships we created. Only when we understand the severe ramifications of justifying, minimizing and rationalizing our offensive behavior do we acquire the willingness to accept our part in the dysfunction that shatters our serenity. When we make our peace of mind non-negotiable, we are able to lay aside our alcoholic code of justice and offer forgiveness to the offending party.

"Vengeance is mine sayeth the Lord." Alcoholics effectively demonstrate the wisdom of this scripture. Vengeance is anger. It is a dubious luxury for non-alcoholics that alcoholics cannot afford. For when we harbor any ill-will, we block ourselves off from the Sunlight of the Spirit and wallow in the shadow of death where the insanity of the first drink returns. And for us to drink is to die. We must forgive if we expect to live long and happily in this world. If we are not willing to forgive the offending party, shame overwhelms us and sweeps us back into the bottle. So we pray for the willingness to forgive. Without forgiveness, we cannot make proper amends. We cannot put out of our minds the wrongs of others. And until we do so, we act out on our will and create more harm.

Prayer is essential to the amends process, for we need a change of heart before we can truly make amends and restore balance to our relationships. If we are reluctant, we pray for the willingness to be willing to make amends, and ask God for the strength to do the right thing, no matter the consequences we may face.

No amends is complete without God. He mends the heart and restores emotional balance to our relationships."

Making amends is a way of life

Oldtimer said, "One of the most important amends we alcoholics must make is an amends with the world in general for the unseen damage we caused in our active alcoholism. We can't account for all of our actions, due to our maniacal drinking habits. There are blackouts and hazy recollections of obnoxious behavior on our part. As such, we can never fully account for the litany of damage we caused our fellow man.

Just as our drinking knew no bounds, our self-centeredness knew no bounds and we caused untold pain, heartache, and misery wherever we ventured. When we commit our lives to AA's primary purpose-to stay sober by helping others to achieve sobriety-we are making an amends that will lead us to assume mastery over alcohol and our instincts for sex, society, and security. This divine purpose gives God dominion over our inner-verse, and He directs our instincts to achieve His divine purposes. Our amends allow us to bring infinite good to the world that will eventually outweigh the damage we caused when we acted as a force of self-will run riot. Our commitment to the primary purpose will drive our choices in all of our affairs. Our choices will drive our actions, and our actions will deliver us into a way of life that gets incredibly more wonderful as time passes.

As we change our life to fit God's purpose, we become agents working toward the advancement of His Creation. We lose interest in our little plans and designs, and gain interest in the well-being and welfare of the sick and suffering alcoholic. When we live the AA program to the best of our ability, we demonstrate God's omnipotence, and we are living our amends to those on our Eighth Step list, as well as others we may not know we harmed. But the greatest benefit of living the AA program is the amends we make with ourselves.

When we amend our behavior to fit the requirements of the Steps, we are insuring our release from a deadly obsession that doomed us to drink against our will, and a fatal attachment to the self-destructive behavior that manifests whenever we place our pleasures before the principles of the program. Where God guides, he provides healing to all who earnestly follow His way of life. By amending our relationship with God, we change the nature of our existence and improve the nature of our relationship with His world."

Think, think, think

Oldtimer said, "Our thoughts are harmless until we provide them with the force of will that creates actions that work for our benefit or against it. In our alcoholism, every drink that brought destruction to our lives was preceded by delusional thoughts that were empowered by our will. We don't necessarily have a drinking problem so much as we have a thinking problem. We cannot think straight about the effects of alcohol on our life.

When it comes to alcohol we think, then we drink. We think then, we drink. We think, then we drink. Sometimes we don't think; we just drink. Such is the insanity of instantaneous gratification that transformed our thought life into an instrument of self-destruction.

When we live life on God's terms, and at God's pace, we are endowed with God's grace. As such, we learn to pause when our thoughts leave us agitated or doubtful. We apply the principles of the AA program and continue to watch for selfishness, dishonesty, resentment and fear.

In practicing the discipline of Step Ten, we learn to enjoy the value of restraint of pen, tongue and self-will. We no longer react to the impulses of our instincts for sex, society and security-instincts that are designed to spontaneously respond to any external stimulus that enters our consciousness. Instead, we pause for reflection. And in the pause, God's grace catches up with us and provides us with the proper response. The pause is the Good Orderly Discipline that fits us for maximum service to God and the people about us. When we increase our effectiveness and understanding of the pause, we become the watcher of our thoughts. In the pause, we are detached from our thought stream, and granted a moment of clarity from our stream of consciousness. In this moment is freedom from the bondage of self granted us. We are then better able to let go of our desires, and let God take away the thoughts that are not in accordance with His will for us.

As we apply the pause in all of our affairs, and allow God's grace to flow into our life, it is in the pause that we are anointed with the oil of His wisdom. Through this wisdom, a psychic change occurs, and our thought life is placed on the plane of inspiration as our old ideas, emotions, and attitudes recede, and grace becomes our way of life. As a result, a change in our stream of consciousness begins to manifest and our thought life transforms from selfishness to selflessness, dishonesty to honesty, fear to faith, and resentment to forgiveness. In this personality change, we find an effective defense against the first drink, and we are blessed to live happy, joyous and free as empowered agents for God's ever-advancing creation."

All are called but few listen

Oldtimer said, "As we continue to improve our conscious contact with God, we intuitively know how to handle situations that used to baffle us. When we are conscious we need to frequently contact God. We pray many times each day: "Thy will, not mine, be done." We pause when agitated (resentment) or doubtful (fear), and ask God for inspiration, the right thought or action. The answer will come, if our house is in order.

Through inventory, we have identified the line of the will. On one side is self-will, which created the wreckage of the past we endeavor to clean up. And on the other side is the will of our new found Friend, who aids us in the reconstruction of a new life. As we continue to watch for the manifestations of selfishness, dishonesty, resentment and fear, we increase our effectiveness and understanding of the use of prayer and meditation. When these shortcomings pop up, we ask God, at once, to remove them, praying "Thy will, not mine be done."

There will be times when we are consumed by our character defects, so we pray only for the willingness to be willing to let go of them. We then let God do with us as He will. For we are now living on the basis of trusting and relying upon Him, and He removes from us the defects of character that block us off from His will. We have prepared ourselves for this purification process by adopting an attitude of willingness and acceptance in Steps Six and Seven. Our willingness to change, and the acceptance of God's call to service, prepares us to receive intuition from our Source. This vital sixth sense is developed as we remove that which blocked us from God, and it continues to improve as we perfect our prayer life and reinforce it with meditation.

We perfect our prayer life by living our prayers. Where there is hatred, we bring love. Where there is injury, we bring forgiveness. Where there is doubt, we bring faith. Where there is despair, we bring hope. Where there is sorrow, we bring joy. And where there is darkness we bring the Sunlight of the Spirit.

In doing God's will, we become His agents, acting upon His ever-advancing creation. He is Infinite Love, Infinite Power, and Infinite Knowledge, and stands ready to provide what we need to carry forth with His perfect plan. Initially, we will be amazed by the open access we have to our Creator. But as time passes, we see He is a part of us, not apart from us. He is as much a part of us as the feeling we have for a friend—love!

When we live in God's love, we experience the miraculous. There is less danger from fear, excitement, anger, worry, self-pity or foolish decisions. We no longer live life to suit ourselves, and live only to please God. We find that the small, still voice we once ignored has become a great source of wisdom by which we live our new life, one day at a time."

Carrying the message is a selfless act of grace

Oldtimer said, "Counter to popular opinion, AA is not a selfish program. It is a selfless program for selfish people. The idea that selfishness is of benefit to the alcoholic is a message foreign to AA that is carried by agents of the disease who know little of the of the roots of our alcoholism, nor the solution AA offers.

We have a fatal selfishness that leads to our demise at the gates of insanity and death. When we step out of ourselves to help other alcoholics we are demonstrating our willingness to grow beyond our selfishness and nourishing our spiritual life. The AA founders gave selflessly of themselves so that we could find the precious gift of recovery. There were great interruptions to their worldly pleasures, but they willingly sacrificed these pleasures for our sake. Their horrid experience with alcoholism led them to love their sick alcoholic brethren, and they placed nothing before carrying the AA message.

Today, we do far less than they for the future generations of alcoholics who are sure to venture into the rooms of recovery? Are we willing to sacrifice gratification of our human instincts to help the sick and suffering alcoholic? Are we sharing the AA message in the rooms, or speaking a foreign recovery dialect born outside of AA?

The founders left the fellowship a great legacy in the program of recovery. Have we cast it aside in favor of more modern methods that fail the alcoholic and dooms them to death? Are our efforts today sufficient to ensure that future generations of AA will find the precious gift of sobriety?

Our very existence in this world depends on an affirmation of this commitment to carry the AA message. We do not recover by living life on life's terms, whereby we selfishly keep our recovery to ourselves. We must live life on God's terms, that we might be rid of our fatal selfishness.

Nothing lives in the Dead Sea because it doesn't have an outlet. It takes in life giving waters, but offers no outlet and keeps its water contained until it grows foul and stinking with the stench of death. So it is with us alcoholics. If we do not give away what we have been freely given, we fall prey to stinking thinking until we perish from stinking drinking.

In God's economy, it is in giving that we receive. And His grace is a saving grace when it flows from one alcoholic to another."

Feeling versus thinking

Oldtimer said, "Alcoholics feel, act, then think. This is why we lack an effective mental defense against the first drink. We feel like taking a drink, so we take the drink. We then think about the consequences that follow our alcoholic spree.

In Alcoholics Anonymous, we have a program of action, not a program of feeling. We act our way into a new way of thinking by following the Steps. In taking Steps One, Two, and Three, there isn't any direct action we take, other than attending meetings and reading to gather information about our affliction and the solution to it.

Steps One and Two are mental conclusions of the heart that lead to the decision in Step Three to follow the directions indicated in Steps Four through Nine, which prepares us for a lifetime of action with Steps Ten, Eleven, and Twelve. Initially, the action of attending a meeting is sufficient to gather the information about the problem and the solution. Once we have this information, we are automatically at the turning point. We can seek God's protection and care with complete abandon through the Steps, or we can delay the inevitable and go on using self-deception, and proceed down a delusional path until the next bout of drinking hopefully provides us with the willingness to follow through with the suggested program of action.

We have no choice in drinking until we make a choice to live life on a spiritual basis. This is not a theoretical concept upon which we ponder and pontificate, but a planned program of action proven to bring about a spiritual awakening that will bring us into conscious contact with God. In following the Good Orderly Directions of the Steps, we take actions that change our life from the inside out. We no longer feel, act and think. We think, act and feel. As a man perceives so does he think. And as a man thinks so does he act.

The Steps reversed our twisted thought processes by having us take actions that change our thinking, which changes our perception of the world in which we live. We move from self-centeredness to God-centeredness. Our world becomes God's world, and common sense becomes uncommon sense when intuition becomes the guiding force in our lives. And when this occurs we will recoil from a drink as if it were a hot flame. We are restored to sanity so long as we stay on the path God blessed."

If we are fearless and thorough from the start the odds of relapse decrease

Oldtimer said, "The problem of the alcoholic centers in the mind, not in the bottle. Our time away from the bottle often acts as a delusion that leads many alcoholics to believe they are well, simply because they are not drinking today. This is a prelude to relapse. Every alcoholic that ever relapsed wasn't drinking the day before they relapsed-a process that started in their mind.

Alcoholics often balk at some of the AA program. Even though we are warned that half measures avail us nothing, many alcoholics choose to take the program in pieces rather than completely giving themselves to the solution to a hopeless state of mind and body. Their hope is that they are not severely afflicted, and that they can recover on their terms. This hope must be smashed if the alcoholic is to completely surrender and find permanent recovery from alcoholism.

The AA founders beg us to be fearless and thorough from the very start. This attitude is the only approach to an illness that is one-hundred percent fatal when left untreated. We have a solution, but none of us like the self-searching, the leveling of our pride, or the confession of our shortcomings which is required for release from a mental obsession that dooms us to consume fatal amounts of alcohol. When we balk at the solution it is the beginning of a relapse, and evidence of the alcoholic insanity that still grips our mind. It exposes the alcoholic ego which is at the core of our addiction to alcohol. It is this part of our mind that balks at examination, lest it be exposed for the fallacy that it is.

The alcoholic ego exists on a lie and works in concert with the alcoholic to oppose the will of God and deny the truth of our condition. Only through rigorous honesty and fearless inventory can we expose the ego and it's delusions. We cannot be afraid of how we look in the eyes of others. What we fail to expose to the light will drag us back into the darkness and to a fatal end. When we give one-hundred percent to this program and leave no stone unturned in our search for the truth, we find ourselves in God's presence, where the miraculous occurs. We are relieved of our obsession and given the power to transform the world about us. This is the power the AA founders discovered which has brought the miracle of recovery to millions who once suffered, as they did, from a hopeless state of mind that doomed them to a fatal end!

Transforming our human instincts to serve God's purpose

Oldtimer said, When we decide to completely give ourselves to the simple program of recovery AA offers, we have decided to live life on God's terms. We failed miserably at life on life's terms, and this led us to life on alcohol's terms. So now we turn our life over to the care and direction of God by applying spiritual tools to every aspect of our life.

We turn our sex life over to God by applying inventory to our past sexual conduct, and trying to live up to God's ideal in our romantic relationships. We satisfy our social instinct in the freedom we find from guilt and shame by making amends with people we have harmed, and by changing our behavior so as not to bring the same harm to others in the future. We can then be alone at perfect peace and ease, and once again look the world in the eye.

We find emotional and material security in the Eleventh Step when we pray for knowledge of God's will for us and the power to carry it out. This protects us from a return to old behavior, and keeps us safe from a return to the old ideas, emotions, and attitudes that governed us in our alcoholism. The pursuit of our primary purpose leads to a choice to live life on a spiritual basis through our use of the kit of spiritual tools that AA provides. This results in actions that build a more abundant life free from the pitiful, incomprehensible demoralization we found ourselves in when we lived life on alcohol's terms.

When our purpose fits God's purpose, we find His grace is sufficient, and we uncover an abundance of spiritual gifts that enrich our life beyond measure-gifts we use to act as agents for God, and fit ourselves to be wholly useful to Him and the people about us."

We clean house in preparation for a Divine Visitor

Oldtimer said, "Alcoholics have mastered the victim mentality. In justifying our maniacal drinking, we sought out anyone and anything to blame for our alcoholic sprees. It could be our spouse, our lover, our kids, our jobs, our life in general. It didn't matter. We focused on something outside of ourselves as the cause of our drinking. It became a constant refrain of poor me, poor me, pour me a drink.

In recovery, we find that this perspective was not limited to just our drinking. It was etched into our thinking. We honed our skill to the point that we had become professional victims, seeking out untrustworthy people in which to place our trust, and seeking unstable situations that brought drama into our lives on a daily basis. Through the inventory process, we found that we created our problems—even though we did not think so. We faced the facts and found that we had made decisions based on self-will, stepped on the toes of our fellows, then blamed them for retaliating.

Inventory shows we were not the innocent victims we portrayed ourselves to be, but the source and instigator of our problems. To rise above our self-proclaimed victim status requires a great deal of house cleaning. We must accept our part in all of our problems and take responsibility to clean up our side of the street. In doing so it becomes apparent that God's grace, mercy and love had been there for us all along. He carried us when we could not carry ourselves, loved us when we could not love ourselves, trusted us when we could not trust ourselves, understood us when we could not understand ourselves, accepted us when we could not accept ourselves;, and forgave us when we could not forgive ourselves.

We were blind to His perfect faith because we chose to be a victim of alcohol rather than victorious over it. Through a spiritual awakening we begin to see the world from an entirely different angle. We accepted our troubles as an opportunity for God to show His omnipotence by working through us to help others. We find that we are no longer victims, but survivors of our own self-destruction, and humbly lay claim to the gift of grace God had intended for us all along.

Through our fallen nature we created space for the miraculous to enter our broken lives, bring healing to our wounds, and lift us up where we belong. We find much of Heaven when we accept the Hell on Earth we created, and atone for our mistakes. We walk the path to victory over alcohol, not as victims of a fatal illness, but as redeemed agents for God, prepared to fully participate in the advancement of His creation."

Our secrets keep us sick until we reveal them to another

Oldtimer said, "Our secrets do not merely keep us sick. They kill us!

Selfishness, dishonesty, resentment and fear are fuel for the engine of obsession that drives us to drink. These defects of character create the dysfunctional behavior that makes our life unmanageable, and a drink that much more attractive. When we fail to bring these maladjustments to the light of truth they keep us restless, irritable and discontented. Under this stress we will seek the chemical peace of mind that comes by taking a few drinks. But since we have an insatiable craving for alcohol, once we take the first drink we are off on another alcoholic spree, and in a short time, confronted with the four horsemen of the Alcoholic Apocalypse—Terror, Bewilderment, Frustration and Despair!

Therefore, it is crucial that the sponsor create an air of confidence with the newcomer through their confidentiality. The sponsor must convince them that anonymity means what they reveal will remain confidential. What is said between two alcoholics forever remains between those two alcoholics. When the newcomer shares their take-it-to-the-grave secrets with their sponsor it becomes the sponsor's take-it-to-the-grave secret. The sponsor must be the closed-mouth friend the newcomer needs to share their innermost secrets, or else they perish drink in hand.

If we cannot, or will not, live up to this grave responsibility required of a sponsor, it is best we send the newcomer to someone who can and will. For it is this confidentiality that frees the newcomer to share that which keeps them bound to the shame of self, and, therefore, the bottle. This is the Divine task for which we are anointed as spearheads of God's ever advancing Creation.

What He has brought together, to serve His purpose, let no man break asunder with loose lips. For it will surely sink the ship upon which all our fortunes rise."

Our broken moral compass guides our misconduct with others

Oldtimer said, "We are like a tornado roaring, through the lives of other people. In the eye of the tornado, it is peaceful and calm. Alcoholics exist in the eye of the tornado. While we are enjoying a blissful, drunken experience, everything around us is suffering the destruction of an alcoholic tornado roaring through their lives.

We are an extreme example of self-will run riot, but we usually don't think so. Our moral compass is broken. It is stuck on stupid, and in our self-centeredness we believe we're not hurting anyone but ourselves. This simply isn't true. We are weapons of mass destruction that bring chaos and confusion into the lives of others, even in our best moments.

In the Fourth, Fifth and Ninth Steps, more is revealed about the destruction we have wrought upon others. In between the action of those Steps, we turn our compass over to God.

As a result of Steps Four we have uncovered our brokenness with an understanding of our need for repair at the hands of the Master. We have discovered those defects of character that we have admitted are objectionable and in need of repair.

In Steps Six and Seven we become willing to have God take them away, root and branch. We offer our compass to God for a course correction that will bring forth a desire to let Him take us to better things. Some of these we may not be entirely willing to turn over to God, so we pray for the willingness to be willing to let them go. When the pain of holding on to them becomes greater that the pain of letting go of our defects of character, we become willing to let go and let God commence repairs.

Steps Six and Seven are merely attitude adjustments, where we let loose of self-sufficiency, and grow into God dependency. We plant the seed of willingness and acceptance in our mind, and the remaining Steps fertilize these seeds that grow into the fruits of purity, unselfishness, honesty and love. Under the radiance of the Sunlight of the Spirit, not only is our moral compass repaired, but we blossom into a new life of which we have never dreamed. We are reborn!"

The discipline of the Steps requires us to be hard on ourselves and considerate of others

Oldtimer said, "When we pray and ask God to make us an instrument of His peace, we need to prepare ourselves for discomfort. God answers our prayer with a transformation that is both wonderful and terrifying. God will remove from us that which is opposed to His peace, and many of our defects of character that block His peace, we still cling to for the comfort they once brought us in the past. But now we find our salvation in the growth and maintenance of a spiritual life. A life we have never experienced that delivers to us an experience with God that gets infinitely more wonderful as time passes.

We need only follow a few simple rules to bring about this miraculous experience. This requires of us great discipline. Under the rule of discipline, we find that our character defects are nothing more than the agents of King Alcohol which try to deny us the peace we seek from God. Therefore, we must make our peace of mind non-negotiable if we expect to live a long and fruitful life of recovery.

We must discipline our alcoholic mind, and this means we must be hard on ourselves and considerate of others. This is difficult for the self-centered alcoholic mind. We have been enslaved to our emotional nature for a long time, and denying our childish nature brings us great discomfort. Selfishness aligns our will against God, and we pursue what we want, when we want it, with the belief that it will bring us comfort. This drive for comfort was the force that drove us to drink to the point of ruin. If we are going to recover from a hopeless state of mind and body, we must realign our powers of denial. We must deny our instincts for sex, society, and security the gratification they desire.

To do so requires us to develop the discipline of prayer. For when these impulses dominate us, and we act on them, they create consequences that make our life unmanageable. If we fail to put them in check, they eventually create within us a restlessness that drives us to seek the ease and comfort of the first drink. Therefore, under the order of discipline, we continue to watch for selfishness, dishonesty, resentment, and fear. These are the impulses of our instincts. So we pray and ask God to remove them.

Through the discipline of prayer, we are transformed by the Spirit and recreated in the image of our Creator. Through this transformation, we gain dominion over our instincts and find the peace of God. We are then fit to better serve Him and the people about us. We become spearheads of His ever-advancing Creation and transmit His grace to the world.

Where there is hatred, we transmit love. Where there is injury, we transmit forgiveness. Where there is doubt, we transmit faith. Where there is despair, we transmit hope. Where there is sorrow, we transmit joy. Where there is darkness, we transmit the Sunlight of the Spirit. We bring the way to truth and life to those in need, and all that we give away becomes the elements of a character forged through discipline, into an empowered agent of God."

Step Eight requires a step into spiritual maturity

Oldtimer said, "We made a list of all the people we had harmed, and became willing to make amends to them all. In Step Eight, willingness is once again put front and center in our recovery. We prayed in Step Seven that God grant us the strength to go forward and do His bidding. This request moves us forward from Step Seven to Steps Eight and Nine.

We have a list of people we have harmed. We made it with our Fourth Step inventory. Towards those whom we held resentment, we found that we had set the ball rolling with our dishonest, self-seeking actions, words, and motives. Through our manipulative behavior, we aroused jealousy, suspicion, and bitterness in others, but we focused only on their acts of retaliation after we had stepped on their toes. Now we are prepared to make amends for our transgressions. We list those we are ready to make amends with immediately, and also those we weren't ready to make amends with. For those we were unprepared to make amends with, we turn them over to God, and once again pray for the willingness to be willing.

In Steps Eight and Nine, we go forward in the spirit of forgiveness. We put out of our minds the wrongs others have done by offering them forgiveness in spite of the apology we didn't receive. This requires spiritual maturity on our part. And by addressing the amends we are willing to make, and praying for the willingness to be willing to forgive those who harmed us so deeply, we attain enough spiritual maturity to eventually tackle the amends we were not willing to make.

Emotional and spiritual maturity does not conform to a schedule, so we seek spiritual growth by applying the prayer and meditation prescribed by the Steps.

Amends means change, and until we have changed the nature of our being, we cannot change the nature of our dysfunctional relationships. Perhaps we still have an overabundance of pride, anger, regret, remorse, or shame that blocks us from moving forward. It has been repeatedly proven that we cannot change our nature without God's help. This is a process under His control. Until we have acquired the requisite willingness to let loose the defects that block us, and forgive the offenses of others, it is foolish to approach those who were complicit in a shared dysfunctional relationship. Doing so destroys our opportunity to carry a beneficial message.

We are acting as agents for God. He orders our steps in these delicate affairs. We ask Him not only how to make the matter right, but also when to make our approach. God knows our heart and the heart of the other person involved. His timing will provide us the best opportunity to mend our fractured relationships in a manner that proves beneficial to both parties."

Amends heals the shame that binds us to alcohol

Oldtimer said, "There is an abundance of shame in an alcoholic's thought process. Rightfully so! We have committed acts that violate God's law and our own moral and philosophical convictions. So powerful is shame's influence on our mind that we will create a false personality to replace our true selves—a personality which we view as flawed. Thus do we begin full flight from reality, and live the life that feels most normal to us—our alcoholic life.

This life is the only one that feels normal to us because we only feel normal when we drink. In our perception, reality is messy, ugly, and inconvenient. It leaves us restless, irritable, and discontented. Thus do we seek our comfort in alcohol.

If we are to recover, we must seek our comfort in the truth. This requires a change in our outlook and perception on life. We must be hard on ourselves and considerate of others if we are to grow in the spiritual life that is our salvation. Every problem we face in life is nothing more than a question of faith. Do we trust God to bring us through the dilemma? Is His grace sufficient? So it is with the Ninth Step.

Is God bigger than our shame, or do we consider our shame to be greater than God? Our reaction to our amends list will tell us just who we think God is, and what we think we are worth.

Is God so limited in our minds that He cannot see us through the task of amends? If that is our thought process we need to change our belief system concerning who God is and what He is capable of doing. Shame will lead us to believe God is limited in His abilities. Therefore, His grace is insufficient and not worth the self-sacrifice our amends requires. So we balk at righting the wrongs we have perpetrated against others.

Sometimes shame manifest as pride, and we convince ourselves we have done nothing wrong, or our misconduct was justified in light of the pain others inflicted upon us. We must put out of mind the wrongs of others, and go to them in a helpful forgiving spirit.

In the spirit of forgiveness, we find freedom from pride and shame. In the spirit of service we find our worth to God and our fellow man. So long as we live in the shadow of shame, we will balk at certain amends and remain in bondage to alcohol. Void of God's grace, our defects of character dominate our thought process, and we continue to live a lie. In this state, when we receive God's grace, we perceive it as a gift of which we are not worthy. This belief system does not deter God from blessing us, but it does keep us in bondage to shame.

Even as we continue to receive His unmerited favor, we refuse to change our beliefs about God and our relationship with Him. Shame would have us believe that God has judged us unworthy, and holds us in contempt for our past acts. Before we can unconditionally accept God's grace, we must accept that He loved us when we were doing our worst because He knew that was the best we could do under the yoke of alcoholism.

As we proceed through our amends list, we find that God's yoke is easy and His burden is light. God didn't create our flawed character molded in shame, but our flawed character can be useful to Him. He uses broken people like us to reach broken people like us. In helping other, we finally find freedom from our bondage to shame, and begin to comprehend and accept God's omnipotence. In righting our wrongs, we find our worth by repairing the wreckage of the past and putting ourselves in service to God and our fellow man."

Clearing the minefield of the alcoholic mind

Oldtimer said, "Step Ten is where we begin to earnestly trudge the road to our happy destiny. This is not an overnight matter. It is a lifetime practice.

In Steps Six and Seven, we adopted an attitude of willingness and acceptance. In Step Six, we became willing to have God take away our character defects. In Step Seven we accepted our flawed character, good and bad, and assisted God in discarding that which does not serve Him. In Step Three, we formed a partnership with God-a new relationship—and now we assist Him in our spiritual transformation.

We fit ourselves to better serve Him by monitoring the atmosphere of our mind and watching for explosive mines that might trip us up and blow up our recovery. When troubled, we recognize that we have an acceptance problem. Some person, place, thing, or situation doesn't meet our expectations, and we respond with selfishness, dishonesty, resentment and fear. Rather than allowing our ego to mindlessly drive us through the minefield, we apply the Three A's—Awareness, Acceptance and Action.

Once we identify the character defects at work, we can determine if acceptance or action is the proper course to take. Either way, prayer is required. We pray for the humility to accept what is unacceptable to us, with the faith that ultimately it serves God's purpose. Or we pray for the courage to take the action necessary to change the situation. God's will always requires courage on our part. In seeking His will, we must maintain a channel of communication with Him who grants us the power to do His bidding. We must turn in all things to the Father of Light, who presides over us all, and ask for the courage to change.

Fear of change is a powerful cement that binds us to our alcoholic life. Faith means courage, and when we pray for the humility to accept a situation, or the power to change it, we are exercising our faith and exorcising our fear. It is in the continual exercising of our faith that our intuition comes to fruition, and we develop a deeper belief in God's way of life.

In all of our affairs, we act as His agents and carry a beneficial message to the world that advances His creation and spurs our own spiritual growth. Thus do we maintain a way of life that gets infinitely more wonderful as time passes."

Our daily bread is delivered one prayer at a time

Oldtimer said, "When we pray the AA way, selfless prayer becomes our habit. One day at a time, we seek the daily bread that nourishes our spirit.

We start our day with prayer, asking God to divorce our thoughts from our self-pity, dishonest and self-seeking motives. It is on the level of motive that we make our choices. Our mind constantly make choices on the deepest level of conscious thought. It is an autonomous function. Often, our instincts drive our choices. This takes us back to the past, where we recall experiences that were pleasant or unpleasant, and from these memories we make the choices that drive the actions that constitute our life.

Sometime, this power of recall brings to our conscious mind the euphoria of alcohol. The pain, suffering and humiliation that drove us to AA is easily pushed aside, and euphoric recall leads us back to the insanity of the first drink. We don't think of the alcoholic spree that is often followed by pitiful, incomprehensible demoralization. We remember only the bliss that alcohol used to deliver with that first drink. Now, we seek to stay sober by building and maintaining a spiritual life.

Every day is a day we must choose to live life on a spiritual basis, or take our chance with the impotence of self-will. Starting our day by turning it over to God in prayer is our best chance for a sober day. As we go through our day, we are sure to experience a lack of faith, and we become agitated or doubtful. After all, we are experiencing life on a level we have never experienced before.

When we play the role God assigns, He enables us to match calamity with serenity, doubt with faith, and hope with despair. We have at our disposal a direct connection to God, and each day we pray the AA way we improve this connection.

God responds to our prayers with the miraculous. Therefore, when agitated or doubtful, we ask God for inspiration, and the right thought or action. This prayer is humility in action, and in humility we find serenity. In serenity our faith is restored and we undergo a rearrangement of our inner-verse which focuses our attention on God rather than our problems. We suddenly realize that God is bigger than our problems.

We have seen and experienced this in AA. When our purpose is God's purpose, His wisdom flows into us and we intuitively know how to handle situations that used to baffle us. We remind ourselves many times each day that we are no longer running the show. Our life is now God's business, and through prayer we accept His guidance in all of our affairs.

Selflessness is the path to serenity. It disconnects us from our selfish instincts for sex, society and security, and connects us to the Infinite Power, Love and Wisdom that flows from God. The less self we contain, the more God we experience. The more God we experience, the greater our faith. The greater our faith, the more miraculous our recovery."

God's grace is abundant in recovery

Oldtimer said, "When we have a spiritual awakening, we enter the World of the Spirit and find that God's grace is sufficient and His abundance overflowing.

As alcoholics, we became addicted to the idea of more. When we were drinking, we needed more and more alcohol to satisfy a craving beyond our control. Even when we get sober, we develop a craving for gratification of our instincts for sex, society, and security, and no matter how much we get what we want we still crave more. These cravings leave us in a state of self-centered fear, and we grab at more of everything for fear of losing it all. No matter how we tried, we could not find contentment in material gain, no more than we found it in our drinking. We are a people obsessed with more. Our instincts are crucial to our survival and identity, but as long as we align our instincts with the ego, we shall always find ourselves wanting.

Now, in recovery, we have a new employer, who provides what we need, so long as we stay close to Him and perform His work well. When we commit to the Steps, we find that we need to stay close to God and serve our fellow alcoholics if we expect to live long and happily in this world. In doing so, we find that our true purpose fills the void within, and we not only have enough material goods, but our instincts can be satisfied with less. We no longer need to the be number one, so long as we are with the One who has all power. His love, grace, and knowledge is sufficient. We find that the lust of our lower nature has been replaced by love of a higher nature. We no longer sexualize the opposite sex, but view them in the Light of the Spirit from which they were created.

We are promised that we will lose our fear of economic insecurity. And this is true. But we also lose our fear of emotional insecurity. Even if our loved ones reject our attempts at reconciliation, we find a host of friends in the fellowship of the Spirit, who love us unconditionally. We suddenly realize that our arrival in AA was a miraculous affair engineered by God. And if He brought us through the hell of our addiction, He won't abandon us in our recovery.

Our instincts serve a purpose in our life, but we were not meant to serve them. We cannot serve two masters. A house divided cannot stand. But if we choose to serve God rather than our instincts, we will find that our needs are abundantly met, and our cup overflows with the bounty of His Grace."

Out of feeling and into action

Oldtimer said, "Alcohol so warped our state of being that we became a slave to our emotional nature. So often, we simply felt like taking a drink. Most times, we put little thought into taking the drink. We felt the desire for the emotional reassurance that comes with that first drink, and so we took it. We learned to overcome our fear via alcohol. We learned to increase our happiness with alcohol. We learned to rise above depression with a drink.

These lessons taught us that emotional gratification takes precedent over all other interests we may have. No matter how great the consequences, we sought the emotional relief that alcohol provided. This enslavement to the emotional boost alcohol gave spread to every other area of our life, and we learned to feel our way through life.

We must learn to act against our emotional nature, and act on spiritual principle instead, if we expect to live long and happily in this world. For if we continue to act out on our feelings above everything else, we will one day feel like taking a drink. And since we are in the habit of doing what we feel like doing, we will bypass any mental defense we have used to prevent us from taking the first drink-a drink that brings us a sense of ease, and comfort and ends in pitiful, incomprehensible demoralization.

One of the first actions we take is designed to break our enslavement to our emotional nature. We are told to change playmates, playgrounds and playthings. There is great emotional attachment to all three, and breaking our bond with them is a major step toward freedom from the bondage of self. Later, we do something totally against our emotional nature—we work the Steps.

There is a reason we balk at undertaking this radical process of change. Alcoholics are undisciplined, and we seek our worldly comfort rather than adhere to the strict regimen the Steps require for their successful consummation. As we follow the Good Orderly Directions AA offers, we rise above our emotional nature and connect with our spiritual nature. Intuition begins to take precedence over gratification of our instincts for sex, society, and security, and living life on life's no longer baffles us. Instead living life on God's terms brings us clarity of thought and charity of the heart as we learn the true meaning of giving to receive.

Our spiritual awakening brings about an emotional realignment, and reason and logic become the guiding forces behind our actions. As a result, our heart and mind are in alignment, and right feelings begin to follow right actions. Rarely do we feel the desire for the drink, for God has restored us to our right mind. Only then can we think our way through the drink, for love becomes the dominant emotion that guides our thoughts and actions. And when we act on love, we no longer participate in the self-destructive habits we developed in our active alcoholism. Instead, we begin the long process of reconstructing a life decimated by drinking and self-will run riot. As we trudge the road to freedom, we find the happy destiny that is God's grace.

It is in giving of ourselves to the Steps that we receive the gift of recovery

Oldtimer said, "We give as we get, and we get as we give. This is the Karma of recovery. If you are miserable in your recovery, it may be that you are not giving freely of yourself.

To give freely means we give of our time, energy, and effort to those who can do nothing for us, and we expect nothing in return. When we expect a specific return we cancel out the Law of Karma and block the blessing that was coming our way. In fact, we may be blind to the blessing because we expect it to come in a certain way, and that is where we place our focus. This is nothing more than self-seeking behavior. We were not being kind and loving with our act of giving; we were doing business. The expectation of a specific result always leaves the alcoholic with a restless spirit, where nothing brings us contentment and everything irritates us.

Placing principles before personalities brings about great interruptions to our pleasures, and great inconvenience.

Crisis never occurs on a schedule, and we must always be at the ready when the sick and suffering alcoholic reaches out anytime and anywhere. Our blessing in the affair is a reprieve from our bondage to self. When we get out of ourselves and offer unconditional service to others, it opens the way for God to enter into our hearts and mind to perform the miraculous transformation that only He can perform.

No one ever overdosed on unconditional love. As we give it to others, we receive it from God. As we get it from God, we give it to others. This rescues us from a fatal selfishness that would have us wallow in a bitter pit of sobriety that saps the joy out of life and plunges us into darkness. We find freedom and release in our fellow alcoholics, who understand the language of the heart which is transmitted through our unconditional service."

Willingness connects us to the Power Source of the Steps

Oldtimer said, "We have been given a kit of spiritual tools with which we shall build a new life in recovery. The Steps are the power tools of AA, and the Power Source is God. When we turn our will and life over to God, we surrender our power unto Him. For the tools to work properly and bring the power we need into our lives, we must be willing to plug into the Power Source, and this is begins with prayer.

In Step Three, we turn our will and life over to the care of God with a prayer. We pray, "God I offer myself to Thee to build with me, and to do with me as Thou will." With this prayer, we are making a contract with God. It is a partnership whereby He provides the direction and power we need, and we provide the action needed in the divine reconstruction of our lives. Before the reconstruction can begin, there must be a deconstruction of our old ideas, emotions and attitudes. So we pray, "Relieve me of the bondage of self, that I may better do Thy will."

There are only two wills in our world: self-will and God's will. We cannot serve two masters, so we pray for release from the old master of self, that we may serve a new Master. This is confirmed when we state our purpose for release from the bondage of self-"to better do God's will." We pray also for God to "take away my difficulties."

Spiritual tools are difficult to apply because our carnal nature balks at spiritual development, and often we Ease God Out and act out on our will. This is our difficulty. The same will that failed to keep our drinking in check, and led to the drama in our life that made alcohol an attractive alternative to life on life's terms, is a barrier to God's will. So we ask God to help us serve Him by removing the binds of our self-serving nature. Through prayer, we put ourselves in service to God and the people about us, that we may grow beyond a fatal self-centeredness.

We ask God that we may "bear witness to those I would help of His Power, His Love and His Way of life." We no longer debate God's existence, but demonstrate His omnipotence with our service to Him and our fellow man. We seal our contract when we pray, "May I do Thy will always." In doing so, we find the power we need to overcome our obsession for alcohol, and our unmanageable life is transformed by God's grace into a selfless beacon of hope for the sick and suffering alcoholic."

Self-reflection uncovers the self-reliance that leads to self-centered fear

Oldtimer said, "We had a new employer. Being all powerful, He provided what we needed so long as we kept close to him and performed His work well." This promise advises us to face and be rid of the things that are blocking us from God.

As long as we let the wreckage of the past occupy our attention we cannot move close to God. Therefore, we undertake a searching and fearless inventory that we might face and be rid of things that act as a barrier between us and God. We have taken ourselves hostage and barricaded the door with pride, anger, guilt, shame, remorse, regret, resentment, fear, etc. These are the maladies of self that serve to keep God out of our life, and when we Ease God Out we find we have kept other people out of our lives as well. So God's work for us is to recognize the problem so that we may find the solution in Him.

We cannot fool ourselves about values. Our pride leads the procession of our deadly defects and blinds us to the destructive effects of self-will. If we are to engage the power of God, we must humble ourselves in the presence of truth, that we may find freedom from our dependence on alcohol. We have a problem that places us beyond human aid. No human power can relieve us of our alcoholism. Any solution we create with our alcoholic thinking is destined to fail, because the mind that created the problem is limited in it's ability, and is incapable of solving the problem it created.

God can solve our alcohol problem if we seek Him with the same vigor with which we sought a drink. We can leave no stone unturned in our pursuit of the Power we need-a Power that rests only in God.

Some say it is foolish to rush into the Steps, but millions have proven what Bill Wilson constantly emphasized: delay is deadly. We must seek God now, for we know not when that certain time will come when we lack an effective mental defense against the first drink. So we rigorously commence our quest for God's power with a personal inventory that will identify the defects of character that keep us bound to self and self to alcohol.

A business that takes no regular inventory usually goes broke. And when we come to AA, we find we are not only broken, we are spiritually bankrupt. So we perform the work God assigns, which will release us from our bondage and grant us the freedom we desire. When we are thorough with the task at hand, we begin to feel the flow of His spirit into us. We find that His yoke is easy, His burden light, and His blessings abundant. For He is a benevolent Employer who grants us the miracle to which we are entitled-miracles He ordains as our birth right, which we cast aside in favor of self-reliance.

Through self-reflection, we find that self-reliance leads to self-centered fear which leads to selfishness, dishonesty, and resentment. When we place our dependence on God instead of self, our fears fall from us, we feel the nearness of our Creator, and we begin to have a spiritual experience that transforms our mind and releases us from the obsession to consume that which is consuming our life."

The truth is the language of the heart every alcoholic needs to share

Oldtimer said, "Rigorous honesty is essential to recovery. It is the basis upon which we build a healthy relationship with God.

For too long, we relied on other people's perception of God, and found only failure. To access God's Power, which the alcoholic desperately needs to live long and happily in this life, we must access the truth about ourselves. In doing so, we gain access to His power. So long as we remain on this axis of truth, we are endowed with an abundance of His grace, and maintain mastery over alcohol. Through this freedom we are blessed with the life God intended for us. By building a trusting relationship with God, based on the truth, we grow in His image and project His light into the world.

To uncover this truth, we must commit ourselves to a lifetime of inventory. A wise man once said, "The unexamined life is a waste. Our alcoholic life is proof of this folly. Rarely did we fail to examine the lives of others and determine what they needed to change in order to fit more comfortably in our lives. Now we take the same keen perception and turn it upon ourselves to identify those things within us that keep us from fitting comfortably into a spiritual life.

A defect of character is any component of our personality that we place before a healthy relationship with God. When we react to fear, anger, guilt, remorse, selfishness, or some other shortcoming, we are placing these maladies before God's will, and the results are always defective. Only when we become entirely ready to allow God to remove them from the forefront of our minds, does His power to flow into our lives.

The alcoholic has moral and philosophical convictions galore, but we cannot live up to these values because we place far too much stock in our character defects and, thus, lack the power to live up to the beliefs of our conscience. When we take our focus off of our defects and place our focus upon God, we access His power, and this allows us to grow in His image, one day at a time."

Failing our way to spiritual success

Oldtimer said, "In AA, we fail our way to success when we incorporate Steps Six and Seven into Step Eleven. When we do so, we grow into an unshakable faith that results in spiritual growth.

In Step Six, we adopt an attitude of willingness to grow along spiritual lines. Even if we are not willing to let go of our defects of character that block our spiritual growth, we pray for the willingness to be willing to change. In this way, our prayer life is directed by our human flaws and our willingness to let God carry us to better things.

In Step Seven, we adopt an attitude of acceptance. We accept our imperfection and God's timing in removing our defects of character. We find that God can use some of our defects of character to serve His purpose. After all, Bill Wilson's defect of grandiosity served God's desire to grow AA beyond it's meager beginnings.

When we pray for knowledge of God's will and the power to carry it out, it reflects our commitment in the Seventh Step Prayer, when we asked God to grant us strength as we go forward to do His bidding. As we trudge forward on the road to happy destiny, we are sure to stumble over our defects of character, and whenever we stumble, we regain our balance whenever we kneel to pray. In this way, do we quickly find our happy destiny in the present moment. We find that frequent contact with the newcomer and each other becomes the highlight of our day, and we increase our understanding and effectiveness of the spiritual process. Self-seeking slips away, and we are in less danger of fear, excitement, worry and self-pity. We do not tire so easily and we become much more efficient, as we no longer try to arrange life to suit ourselves. We lose our fear of today, tomorrow, and the hereafter as our fears fall from us and we begin to feel the nearness of our Creator. We wear the world as a loose garment, and our whole outlook and attitude will shout that we are happy, joyous, and free as we enter a fourth dimension of existence. of which we have never dreamed."

The Seven Deadly Sins and the alcoholic mind go hand in hand

Oldtimer said, "The Seven Deadly sins are character defects that define stinking thinking in the alcoholic. Whenever we live in self-centered fear, pride, anger, greed, gluttony, envy, lust and sloth define our character. These defects are a way of life for one who suffers from alcoholic thinking.

Pride stems from our low self-esteem. We alcoholics are full of self-loathing, so we pump ourselves up with false beliefs about ourselves to project an image of superiority to counter our fear of not measuring up.

Anger is nothing more than an extension of fear. Our fear is that some past injury is about to come upon us once again, so we act out with aggression.

Greed and gluttony are the twin manifestations of selfishness. We fear there isn't enough of anything, so we grasp at more of everything in order to allay our fear of scarcity.

Envy stems from a lack of gratitude for what we have, and a fear that we will not get what we think we deserve. As a result, we covet the possessions of others with the belief that if we have what they have, we will feel what we think they feel. This habit of comparing our insides to others outsides leaves the alcoholic in a state of constant discontentment.

Lust is our attachment to the physical world and the carnal pleasures it contains. The alcoholic pleasure center needs constant stimulation, especially when the alcoholic is not drinking. We are as addicted to external sensory gratification as we were to alcohol, and we will often sacrifice anything of good value to attain it.

Sloth is thought to be when one has a disdain for order and cleanliness, and is manifest in one's unkempt outward appearance. While this may be true, the real source of sloth is an unkempt inner spirit that suffers from neglect. As it is inside, so it is outside.

The alcoholic is on dangerous ground when these defects dominate our thinking. We cannot be rid of them, but we can make spiritual progress and outgrow them by practicing a rigorously honest program of mindfulness where we continue to watch for selfishness, dishonesty, resentment, and fear, and ask for God for help in removing them from our lives. God can, and will, help any alcoholic who earnestly seeks a better life. We need only surrender to His way of life-the way of happiness, joy and freedom."

Admitting our wrongs brings God into our life

Oldtimer said, "Insofar as the alcoholic is concerned, the wisdom we seek in the Serenity Prayer is the ability to know the difference between the results produced by self-will, and the results produced by God's will. Our abundance of past failures provides us with ample evidence of the folly of self-will. Yet it takes great faith and trust in God to learn of the wisdom inherent in His will.

For one with an alcoholic mind, the most difficult challenge we face is admitting our wrongs. Yet only by doing so can we escape the toxic cycle of self-destruction we create in our relationships. Admitting we are wrong feels like death to the alcoholic ego, yet it is this same admission that delivers us from the pit of Alcoholic Hell and puts us on the high road to a happy destiny. Only when we have sufficient belief in the positive results our admission can bring, do we become willing to make such an admission.

The needed evidence is in our First Step experience, where we took our initial faltering step into recovery. With the admission of powerlessness over alcohol, we actually escaped the fatal finality of alcoholism. Without this admission, we would have continued on the low road of futility, onto the gates of insanity and death. So in spite of our feelings, we made our admission of defeat. Afterward we found hope in the Second Step when we coupled our admission with a willingness to believe a Power greater than ourselves that could restore us to sanity. We went even deeper by committing our life to this Power, listing our wrongs, and admitting the exact nature of them in Steps Four and Five. We then admitted that we were willing to have our defects of character removed, and acknowledged that we could not do so ourselves when we practiced Steps Six and Seven.

In Steps Eight and Nine, we listed, in detail the targets of our wrongs, and admitted our transgressions to those we have harmed. With the experience of the previous Steps, we have opened a channel to God's peace, and we are well-prepared to reap the abundance of God's power that awaits us when we continue to take personal inventory and promptly admit our wrongs. This practice is the daily dying of self that precedes our awakening into the way of eternal life. It is in the admission of our wrongs that we are reborn in the light of truth, grace, and forgiveness, and gain entrance into the World of the Spirit."

Restoring the corrupted will of the alcoholic

Oldtimer said, "We must turn in all things to the Father of Light, who presides over us all. This is the essence of our new relationship with our Creator. In all things, big and small, we seek His will over our corrupted will. This is essential in the Ninth Step. We have brought great harm into the lives of others. We know not the true damage we inflicted upon, them and our mere presence opens the wounds we inflicted upon them. They may respond to us with vitriol and anger. How we respond to them will determine the nature of our amends. So we pray beforehand and ask God to bless them with His healing grace, and to grant us the understanding we lacked when we created the harm.

We are experts at creating harm. Even in our best moments, we are creators of chaos and confusion. Such is the nature of our self-centered will run riot. We may, at times, have been kind, considerate, modest, generous, patient and self-sacrificing. But in our corrupted state, these desirable qualities became the weapons of mass destruction that cut the deepest wounds in those who loved and trusted us. So long as our motives are linked with self-will, these most virtuous assets become weapons of war alcoholics wage against themselves. We are full of self-loathing, and those who dare to love us become collateral damage in this war.

It is a war we cannot win, so we turn to the One who has all power, and surrender to His will. And it is in His will that we find a love that brings us the peace and understanding that we transmit in our amends. We go forth in a spirit of forgiveness, acknowledging our part in the dysfunctional relationship, and let the aggrieved party set the terms for what they need from us to heal. We then do our best to live up to the terms they set. And every day we do so, we bring healing to ourselves as we live a life of integrity that we always desired, but lacked the power to achieve.

Alcohol sapped this power from us when it corrupted our will. Now, God restores the power, and no longer do we crawl in the gutters of self-pity and shame, but look the world in the eye and walk in God's grace as an agent of His benevolence!"

The solution to alcoholism centers in the the Steps

Oldtimer said, "One day at a time, we continue to watch for the manifestations of self that defeated us. Many of us are baffled at our alcoholic demise. We place the focus on our drinking, and consider abstinence from alcohol as the solution to our drinking problem. But our drinking problem runs much deeper than that. The problem of the alcoholic centers in the mind. Every relapse that returned us to drinking was proceeded by old thoughts and old behaviors that focused on the gratification of our instincts for sex, society, and security. When we come to AA we are encouraged to change playmates, playgrounds, and playthings, and find new friends in the fellowship. These physical changes are only a prelude to the vital change we must undergo. There is a greater change that must occur if we are to maintain our status in the fellowship of Alcoholics Anonymous.

Even after a long period of sobriety, we are prone to the stinking thinking that leads to stinking drinking.

We cannot rest on our laurels. Every day is a day we continue to watch for the states of mind that precede our drinking. Selfishness, dishonesty, resentment, and fear are the mercenaries of the four horsemen of the alcoholic apocalypse. Terror, bewilderment, frustration, and despair are sure to visit us if we fail to deal with their mercenaries in a prompt manner. We continue to watch for selfishness by pursuing selflessness. We continue to watch for dishonesty by pursuing honesty. We continue to watch for resentment by pursuing forgiveness. And we continue to watch for fear by pursuing faith. We do not spend our energy on avoiding the old, but instead we spend our energy on creating the new. This is the proper use of the will.

The problem of the obsession is removed when we apply **G**ood **O**rderly **D**iscipline to the **G**ood **O**rderly **D**irections we have been given. In order to maintain the new order between ourselves and alcohol, we have to grow in our new relationship with God. With our focus placed on the purity of our thought life, our defects of character fall from us— we grow in the image of our Creator, and remain safe and protected from the thoughts that might lead us astray from the path of recovery.

Cultivating serenity through inventory, prayer and meditation

Oldtimer said, "Meditation cultivates our mind to receive the wisdom of God, which comes in the serenity produced by the actions we take with inventory and prayer. The purpose of our inventory is to establish a new relationship with our Creator. We may have been atheist, agnostic, or religious, but our old understanding of God provided an inadequate relationship. If this were not so, we would not drink. Now, through the process of the Steps, we uncover, discover and discard the wreckage of our past life, and cultivate a new connection the with One who has all Power.

We have begun to develop and grow a new relationship with God that really works! When we clear away the wreckage of the past, which stood as a barrier before God, we felt His power flow into our lives. This power changed the nature of our character, and this change in character changed the nature of our relationship with God and the people in our orbit. We lost our dependence upon resentment, and gained dependence on forgiveness. We lost our dependence upon pride, and gained a greater dependence on humility. Envy and jealousy fell by the wayside, and contentment and trust entered our hearts. Selfishness is replaced with selflessness as we continued to pray the AA way.

Sloth gives way to an active desire to pack all we can into the stream of life. Our comfort level with the truth improves, and our practice of dishonesty now brings us discomfort. The fear that distorted our reality falls away, and the Great Reality of the spiritual dimension begins to manifest in our life. Through prayer, mediation, and inventory we open a channel to God's peace and gain access to His Infinite Love, Grace, and Wisdom. Our cups overflow with His grace, and we transmit what we receive from God to those about us. We bring peace where there is disharmony and chaos. We bring love where there is hatred. We bring forgiveness where there is vengeance. We bring faith where there is doubt. We bring hope where there is despair. We bring joy where there is sorrow. For we have become the light that points the way to the truth and life!

We are reborn in God, and the obsession for alcohol has become a figment of the past. One day at a time, we live God's way of life and demonstrate to others His benevolence. We alcoholics, who had fallen beyond the reach of human assistance, found God's unmerited grace in the selflessness of the AA way of life. We gave up on the destructive power of alcohol, and in its place gained a power that restores our sanity and glorifies God."

In anonymity we transmit the love of AA to the sick and suffering alcoholic

Oldtimer said, "When anyone anywhere reaches out for help with their fatal malady, we are responsible for reaching out to them with the AA solution. We have recovered, and have been given the power to help other alcoholics to recover. And for this we, who have received the miracle of recovery, are responsible for those God sends our way. He took the mess that was our life, and transformed it into a message of redemption so that we might bring hope to the hopeless, strength to the weak, and faith to the fallen.

No obstacle can be too great, no situation too challenging in carrying forth with this great responsibility. No day can be too long and our phone may ring in the dead of the night, but we must always keep in mind the fear we had when we reached out of loneliness of the alcoholic pit, seeking help we weren't sure would be there for us.

There will be interruptions to our pleasures, but we find a greater pleasure watching God work the miraculous in the life of another wretched soul who thought they were beyond redemption. We must always take care, and not to lay claim to God's work. So in anonymity we toil, giving all credit to our Creator, who delivered us from bondage.

We must keep in mind that anonymity is trust. We are entrusted with the anonymity of the newcomer when we carry the message to them. This trust is essential if they are to recover. We hold their recovery, and thus their lives, in our hands. No task is greater for the alcoholic.

Anonymity is power. God's power flows through us so long as we try not to lay claim to such power. To do so would diminish its impact and impede its flow to those who need it most.

Anonymity is love. Out of love we hold in confidence that which an alcoholic shares with us. We are prepared to take to the grave their secrets which they planned to take to their grave.

Anonymity is freedom. We free other alcoholics from the chains of alcohol and the bondage of self, that they may experience the same freedom we found when someone held in anonymity our secrets and set us free to live, free to love, free to forgive and be forgiven!"

When it comes to value, alcohol is worthless and the Steps are priceless

Oldtimer said, "Alcoholics are notorious for underestimating the impact of alcoholism and overestimating the power of their mind. The main problem of the alcoholic centers in the mind, but we have a mind that doesn't think so.

In the drinking history of every alcoholic is a failed attempt to control their drinking by force of will alone. Even though this tactic has proven woefully insufficient, we return, over and over again, to our metal prowess without realizing we are working with a defective mental instrument that cannot discern the true from the false. This is the alcoholic dilemma. We may be functional in other areas of our life, but we use this functionality to distort reality to prove we are not alcoholic. We have all the answers, but we are taking the wrong test. It's as if we studied for algebra when the test covers English literature. It is a total misuse of brain power.

The dilemma is further compounded when the alcoholic finds some success at abstaining from alcohol for a while. Eventually, their keen alcoholic intellect convinces them that they have their drinking problem licked, and they take their focus off of not drinking. When this happens insanity returns, and the alcoholic can no longer see and act on the truth about alcohol. A return to drinking ensues and compounds this lack of focus, and the cycle of self-destruction renews in earnest. Even if the alcoholic maintains focus on not drinking, their dishonest mind will convince them the situation wasn't that bad, and that they have been making too big a deal out of nothing. Therefore, the alcoholic sees no value in the spiritual life AA offers as a solution to their drinking problem.

We are powerless over alcohol because of a defective mind that cannot permanently accept the fact that it is incapacitated when it comes to drinking. This is why we cannot provide an effective mental defense against the first drink, a drink that dooms us to consume fatal amounts of alcohol due to a craving beyond our control. This is why we must enlist the aid of a power greater than human power to affect a change in the way we think, feel, and react to life. If we are to live long and happily in this life, we cannot fool ourselves about values.

Alcohol offers us a way of death. God is the way to truth and life more abundant. When we accept God's way of life and pursue the truth of our existence, we establish conscious contact with our Creator, and it this divine connection that transforms our mind. Only when we have had this vital psychic change can we hope to overcome our obsession with alcohol, which delivers us death one drink at a time.

God can and will restore us to sanity and deliver unto us a life that gets infinitely more wonderful as time passes. We need only earnestly follow Him along the path laid out before us in the Twelve Steps!"

Complete surrender brings permanent sobriety

Oldtimer said, "Surrender means we completely give ourselves to the AA program in the same way we surrendered our will and life to alcohol. We let nothing come between us and our desire for a drink. Therefore, we must give the same commitment to recovery.

In Step One, we surrender our drinking. In Step Two, we surrender our thinking. In Step Three, we surrender to God's way of life by applying Steps Four through Twelve to our life. We must completely give ourselves to the Steps if we expect to live long and happily in this world.

This surrender is not an overnight matter. It is a practice that we must continue for a lifetime. For we are never cured of our illness—we only receive a reprieve from the mental obsession one day at a time. We have tried countless vain measures to overcome our mania for alcohol, with very little success. It is for this malady that AA offers a proven solution. If you want what we have, and are willing to go to any lengths to get it, then you are ready to live on a spiritual basis.

We are not asked to have blind faith in making this decision. Countless alcoholics will bear witness to the effectiveness of the AA program before the Third Step decision is made. It is their experience with the AA way of life that strengthens the message of hope that AA offers to the sick and suffering alcoholic. Half-measures avail us nothing, nor does a ninety-nine percent effort. We must give one-hundred percent effort one-hundred percent of the time if our surrender is to produce permanent sobriety. Whatever we place in front of our recovery will be the first thing we lose when we relapse. Our disease is present so long as long as we are thinking.

Alcoholism centers in the mind. It is a subtle foe that distorts the impulse to drink behind seemingly benign thoughts that lead us to balk at some parts of the program. We are not always going to be inspired to walk the path of recovery. Therefore, we must acquire **G**ood **O**rderly **D**iscipline, which will carry us to our happy destiny in our most difficult moments with the faith that where God guides, He provides.

No God no peace. Know God know peace

Oldtimer said, "When we **E**ase **G**od **O**ut of the decision making process the ego takes over and we begin to live life by self-propulsion. We become a weapon of mass destruction that brings chaos, confusion and catastrophe into the lives of others. We are the actor who must run the whole show in hopes of finding internal comfort by rearranging their external environment. We sought our comfort in drink, but after we put the drink down, we seek our comfort in fixing, managing, and controlling our external environment. This is the nature of the ego. It tells us that when everything falls in place we will find peace. Rarely does the ego's plan work because rarely does everything fall in place. Therefore, rarely do we find peace when we **E**ase **G**od **O**ut and pursue life on life's terms.

There is One who has all the power and peace we need to live long and happily in this world. No God, no peace. Know God, know peace.

Our drinking progressed to the point where the chemical peace of mind we once found in the bottle now eludes us. Whereas, we could rely on escape from our cares, concerns, and worries by taking a few drinks, we are now at a stage where there is no situation in our life that a drink cannot make worse. If we are to recover, we must fire the insane manager that brought us to the point where our problems have become astonishingly difficult to solve. That manager is our ego. The part of our mind that is opposed to God. It's management style, self-sufficiency, has brought us to the point of emotional, psychological, and spiritual bankruptcy. Only God can restore us to sanity and lead us in our efforts to successfully reconstruct our lives. When we pray that He build with us and do with us as He will, we are forming a partnership with God where He provides guidance, power, and love in the measure we need it.

He is the Director, and we are the actor playing the role He assigns. He is the Principal, and we are His agents empowered to do His business. He is the Father, and we are His children, whom he loves when we are at our worst, because He knew we were doing the best we could under the yoke of a spiritual malady.

When we turn our will (thinking) and life (actions) over to God, we begin to make choices that bring peace and comfort into our lives. We find that His yoke is easy, and His burden is light. We become an instrument of His peace when we fit ourselves to be of maximum service to Him and the people about us. We heal the hatred within us and transmit love to those about us. We heal our own injuries and transmit forgiveness. We release our doubt and transmit a newfound faith. We overcome our despair and transmit hope. We overcome sorrow and transmit joy. We step out of the darkness of the ego, and transmit the Sunlight of the Spirit. Thus do we become an agent of God, transmitting the grace we have received to those we encounter in His ever advancing creation."

The discipline of inventory offers many life giving benefits

Oldtimer said, "One of the benefits of inventory is the release that comes from moving troubling situations out of our head and putting them down on paper. This gives us clarity about the situation and gives us clarity about the insanity of self to which we are in held in bondage.

When we put our troubles on paper and move them away from the alcoholic scale of justice we carry in our mind, we are able to look at them from an entirely different angle and discover that the source of our difficulties lies within our thinking. We take our troubles out of the dynamics of our magnifying alcoholic mind so that we can take an objective view of them and squarely identify the nature of our wrong in every troublesome situation. In every situation, we find that we are the common denominator in all of our problems.

When we apply inventory to our lives, we put out of our mind the wrongs of others, and accept responsibility for our troubles. As a result, our relationship with our Creator improves because we no longer blame Him for the problems we, ourselves, have created. Through the application of inventory, we have identified the line of the will. There are only two wills in this world: self-will and God's will. One is dominated by the ego, and the other by Spirit. In identifying the line of the will, we have a reliable compass by which to judge our behavior. When we recklessly pursue gratification of our instincts for sex, society, and security, we have aligned ourselves with the ego and are heading for trouble.

God does not want us to be without sexual fulfillment, emotional bonding, and material security. He wills these things in our life in a disciplined manner that will bring comfort to our newfound spiritual status. Discipline is the key to attaining that which we desire. Our alcoholic nature has left us undisciplined, and when we seek our comfort through our instincts, we often do so at great risk to our sobriety.

"Thy will not mine" is the great equalizer between demands of the ego and desires of the Spirit. We cannot drink when we are in God's will. However, when we are under the influence of the ego, our chances of drinking increase exponentially. The line of the will, therefore, is the line that separates us from drunkenness and sobriety. Through inventory, we are able to identify dysfunctional behavior that would bring harm to ourselves and others. Our past behavior becomes our best teacher, and when we learn the lessons the past has to teach us, we are able to choose wisely the course our life shall take.

We can take the low road that the ego offers, and the troubles that have always followed such a choice. Or we can choose the high road of the Spirit and trudge our way to a happy, joyous and free life. Over time, we find that inventory is a valuable spiritual tool that allows us to rise above our troubles and stay sober under any and all conditions."

The wisdom to know the difference is revealed when we uncover the truth

Oldtimer said, "In recovery, wisdom is knowing the difference between the results produced by self-will, and the results produced by God's will. Our past failures provide ample evidence of the destructive impact that self-will had on our life. It takes faith and trust in God to take the action that will allow us to learn of the wisdom inherent in His will.

For the alcoholic mind, the most difficult challenge we face is admitting our wrongs. Yet only by doing so can we escape the toxic cycle of self-destruction we create by running our life on self-will. Admitting we are wrong feels like death to our ego, yet it is only through this admission that we put ourselves on the high road that leads to a happy destiny. Only when we have sufficient belief in the positive results that come from the admission of our wrongs do we become willing to make such an admission.

The needed evidence is in our First Step experience, where we took our initial faltering step into recovery. With the admission of powerlessness over alcohol, we actually escape death. Without this admission, we would have continued on the low road to the gates of insanity and death. So in spite of our feelings, we admitted we were wrong about our relationship with alcohol, and accepted our inability to see and act on the truth about alcohol and ourselves. Our lives were unmanageable because we could not admit our wrongs and repeated the same failed behaviors expecting different results.

We found hope in the Second Step, where we coupled our admission of powerlessness with belief in a power greater than ourselves that could restore us to the truth we could not see. We went even deeper by making a decision to turn our will and life over to this power, listing our wrongs and admitting the exact nature of them in Steps Four and Five. We then admitted that we were ready to have our defects of character removed, and acknowledged that we could not do so ourselves when we practiced Steps Six and Seven.

In Step Eight and Nine, we listed in detail the nature of our wrongs and admitted our transgressions to those we harmed. With the experience of the previous Steps, we are released from shame, guilt, regret, and remorse when we accept our wrongs and make restitution to those who suffered the consequences of them. As a result, we are well-prepared to reap the abundance of God's power, which awaits us when we continue to admit our wrongs on a daily basis. This is the daily dying of self that precedes our awakening into the way of eternal life."

Our defects of character is like a box of chocolates

Oldtimer said, "Life is truly like a box of chocolates, and we turn it over to God, piece by piece. We will freely give to God the pieces we don't like, while holding on to the candy we like.

Step Six asks us to only be willing to let go of our character defects. Rarely is an alcoholic entirely ready to let loose of them all. We will not let go and let God, so long as we derive some pleasurable use from a defect. So we are asked to pray for the willingness to let go, and let God take away those things we have admitted are objectionable. They may be objectionable to our spirit, but so long as the flesh derives pleasure from it, we can put up with the spiritual turbulence. At least, that's what our alcoholic mind thinks.

Just like alcohol, these defects require a steady diet of rationalization, justification and minimization from us in order for us to derive the comfort and pleasure we desire. Of all of the pieces of candy in our box, sex is the last piece we are willing to hand over to God. Just as a child will eat so much candy that it makes them sick, we will act out on our sex instinct until it makes us sick and robs us of our peace of mind. In this discontented state of mind, sex, nor any other comfort device, will suffice, and we seek that imitation peace keeper—alcohol. We are warned that if our sex conduct continues to harm others, we are quite sure to drink. Many alcoholics have paid the ultimate price when they failed to heed this warning.

If we are to recover, there can be no reservations about the program whatsoever. For alcohol is cunning, baffling and powerful. It rearranged our thoughts, emotions and attitudes into a warped delusion of self-centered reality. When we find ourselves defending delusional actions, we are well on our way to another drink of terror, bewilderment, frustration, and despair, with or without alcohol.

Dry drunks, who give half-measures to the AA program, litter the rooms of recovery. They dump their garbage in a meeting in a half-hearted attempt at honesty, while living a dishonest lifestyle. God can and will restore us to emotional sanity free of selfishness, dishonesty, resentment, and fear, if we only seek Him. We need not search in vain, for the path to a new life is given to us in the Steps. And as we take the Steps and draw near to Him, he reveals Himself to us in the face of our fellow man. When we have achieved this vision it can be said that we have achieved emotional sanity."

Step Seven is a commitment of the heart

Oldtimer said, "In Step Seven, as in Step Three, we commit our lives to service. Having persevered with the rest of the program, we have a much better understanding of ourselves, and we now know God much better. We know who we are and Whose we are, and we have begun to develop the elements of a new relationship with our Creator. We unreservedly placed ourselves and our well-being fully into His hands. We have listed and analyzed the terrible destructiveness we created in our life and the lives of others, with our effort to live by self-will alone.

No one has ever made a bigger mess with free will than the alcoholic. Now, we earnestly seek an alternative lifestyle based on God's will. When we do God's will, we see His work in our life and the lives of others.

By now, we have already begun to experience spiritual growth. Despair has been replaced with hope. Faith has helped us to outgrow our fears. Anger has abated, and peace has become a most valuable treasure. We were restless and discontented, but now we lay by the still waters of our Creator and experience a serenity in our soul. We have unburdened ourselves of some of the most troubling defects of character we carried, but we must go much further if we expect to live long and happily in this life. So in prayer, we re-commit ourselves to God.

"My Creator, I am now willing that you should have all of me, good and bad. I pray that you now remove from me every single defect of character, which stands in the way of my usefulness to you and my fellows. Grant me strength as I go out from here to do your bidding."

Step Three was a decision to commit our thinking and actions to God. In Step Seven, we commit our heart to our Creator. We lay aside our burdens and allow him to level the load. We carry only what is useful to Him, and only for as long as He would have us carry it. Our job is to accept ourselves as we are, and keep our feet on the road to a happy destiny. We find that His yoke is easy, and His burden is light. God doesn't ask more of us than we are able to carry with His assistance. Where He guides, He provides, so we trust God will provide what we need to meet the daily challenges life brings us.

By living life on God's terms, we are easily able to meet the challenge of life on life's terms. We find that in every difficult situation, we will receive a blessing or a lesson. We fully recognize that, of ourselves, we are less than zero. By self-will, we add nothing to life, but subtract from it. By God's will, we multiple His grace, until it overflows from our life, into the lives of others we encounter. Thus do we demonstrate His omnipotence in all of our affairs."

Our spiritual growth is essential to the amends process

Oldtimer said, "Before we make our amends list, a change in attitude is required. We go to those we have harmed with a helpful, forgiving spirit. We no longer practice self-seeking. Instead, we accept the world as it is and focus on what needs to be changed in us.

We find that it is in giving that we receive. It is in forgiving that we are forgiven. It is in the daily dying of self that we are born into eternal life. We keep what we have by giving it away. This selfless attitude is the foundation of our amends. Amends means change, and our approach to life is to practice selflessness in all of our affairs.

Selfishness and self-centeredness is the root of our illness. We must be rid of this malady if we are to grow spiritually and live long and happily in this life. One demonstration of the selflessness the AA program demands is working with other alcoholics. In doing so, we take out insurance against the first drink, and this insures that every amends we make is on solid ground.

When we help another alcoholic, it is our living amends towards the world and ourselves. It also accelerates our pace on the road to a happy destiny. This is God's prescription for our hopeless state of mind and body. When we move beyond the selfish motives that caused us to harm others, we begin to recognize that we reap what we sow. As we forgive others, we sense God's Spirit flow into us, and realize we have opened a divine channel by which we receive His forgiveness. Such is the nature of God's economy. When we surrender to God, His power flows in and fundamentally transforms us. This is the daily dying of self that must occur if we are to grow spiritually.

We let go of our selfish ideas, emotions and attitudes by not acting on them. We then pray for God to remove them, and practice selflessness in all of our affairs. Where we have been selfish, we bring charity. Where we have been resentful, we bring forgiveness. This change is the essential amends we make to everyone on our Eighth Step list. Where we have been fearful, we act on faith. Where we have been dishonest, we act with integrity. Where we have been resentful, we act with forgiveness.

Our character defects led us to harm others, and paved our way to the alcoholic pit. God's way of life gave us an exit from the hell of our own making, and it is in exiting this hell that brings about a heavenly experience. So long as we trudge the road of happy destiny, our fear of today, tomorrow, and the hereafter falls from us, and it is this experience that transforms our relationship with others."

Amends is a lifetime process

Oldtimer said, "Remaining sober is an essential element in our amends to our loved ones. If we are not sober, we cannot approach them in the spirit of helpfulness and forgiveness, and carry through with the restitution they deem necessary to heal the relationship.

Therefore, proper prayer and meditation is essential to our sobriety. In prayer we ask God what we should do about each specific matter. We have been selfish in all of our affairs, and if we are to build a new life with our fellow man we must find freedom from the bondage to the selfishness that led to the harm we inflicted on others.

Amends means change. And in our newfound freedom from bondage, we restore balance to our relationships. We bring an end to the dysfunction that has characterized them by bringing an end to the character defects and behavior that once defined them. With God as our guide, we attempt to transform abusive relationships full of pain, heartache and despair. So long as God is in the center of our life, we create inclusive relationships with our family, friends and associates.

In making amends we don't merely admit our wrongs and apologize for our actions. We must follow up our words with kind, thoughtful actions, and attentiveness to the needs of others. In our new approach to life, we must be hard on ourselves and considerate of others. After all, they are risking great emotional, psychological, physical, financial and spiritual devastation when they choose to let us into their lives. But most of all we must confirm our amends on a daily basis by pursuing the vision of God's will for us in all of our affairs.

Our very lives may depend upon the constant thought of others. This is an essential element of every amends we make. We were a black hole of selfishness that sucked the light out of those who happened to enter our life. Now, as agents for God, we bring light where there is darkness. This may require us to play the Good Samaritan everyday. We must be willing to take the lead in making retribution for harms we inflicted upon others. This is done through a commitment to the disciplines of Steps Ten, Eleven and Twelve. By adopting the AA way of life as our own, we maintain our sobriety and bring stability, peace and serenity to all of our relationships.

By continuing our personal inventory, we remain vigilant, and watch for the behavior that stems from attachment to our defects of character. We continue praying for God to remove them whenever they crop up.

By developing the discipline of prayer and meditation, our thoughts are placed on an altruistic plane, and we reflect the same love and care we have receive from our Creator. As His agents, we reach out to other alcoholics with a message that brings redemption to them and ourselves. In giving away what was freely given us, we insure our sobriety and confirm our commitment to the amends we have made.

Gratitude or resentment

Oldtimer said, "Alcoholics gravitate between resentment and gratitude. One of these will leave us at peace, while the other leaves us restless, irritable and discontented. God only wants us to be happy, joyous, and free. He did not intend for recovery to be a glum affair. He has given us the tools by which we build a life of purpose and promise. But it is contingent upon us to remove from our lives the elements of our alcoholic life.

Every day is a day when we must carry the vision of God's will into all of our activities. Resentment occurs when we bring issues from the past into our new way of life. We are triggered by something in the present that brings up an emotional state from the past. When in a resentful state of mind, we are in danger of seeking a shortcut to peace via chemical means. Unless we can accept the state of affairs as they currently are, we can't have peace of mind. And it is only in the peaceful mind that God's presence comes to us.

Gratitude is born of an awareness of God's love, which constantly showers over us. With this awareness, we come to understand His grace and mercy. His mercy is demonstrated by the fact that we survive one day at a time with a fatal illness that has claimed the life of untold millions of alcoholics This existence allows us to fully experience the ebb and flow of life.

Life, in and of itself, is God's grace. When we accept it as sufficient, we receive an abundance of a peace that is not of this world. This experience is the sanity that makes it impossible to hold onto resentments. It is God's grace that makes it possible to see our enemies as sick people that we treat with love and tolerance. And when we do so, they are no longer our enemy, but spiritually sick brethren who we seek to bring the peace we have found. Loving thine enemy is living with grace in accordance with God's will. It brings peace and gratitude to the troubled soul of the alcoholic, and empowers us to help others through their troubles.

When we are living in gratitude, we are acting as agents for God, and we represent the best the Father of Light has to offer."

Selfless prayer becomes our way of life.

Oldtimer said. "We learn to pray the AA way as we proceed through the Steps. Within every Step, from Three through Eleven, lies the elements of the selfless prayer that brings us freedom from the bondage of self. Selfless prayer is the key element that brings about our spiritual transformation. For those who are trying to grow and maintain a spiritual life, the removal of the self-identification we have built and refined must be removed or transformed.

For years alcohol defined our life experience. And with each alcoholic spree, we moved further from our true self, into the valley of shame, where death's shadow haunted us with every drink we took. After every alcoholic spree, we emerged with a greater sense of regret, remorse, and shame for the atrocities we committed in our alcoholic stupor. Fear kept us from taking an honest look at the problems our drinking created, and pride told us there wasn't a problem with our drinking. Other people were to blame. If they would only do as we wished, life would be wonderful, and we would not need to drink to escape their foolishness. They made our lives unmanageable, therefore our drinking was justified.

In this delusional whirlwind we created a false persona that we projected to the world. We craved a certain reputation, but knew deep in our hearts that we did not deserve it. Only when the truth came crashing in on us in the form of a crisis we could no longer postpone or evade, did we muster the courage to take an honest look at ourselves. Deep inside, we recognized a need for change, but only when we came to AA did we know the depth of change that was required to improve our lot in life.

We also learned of the Steps we would need to take to bring about the psychic change necessary to recover from a hopeless malady and regain the essence our true selves. If a new alcohol free life was to come forth, the old life had to be uprooted. This meant the destruction of the false persona we created in our retreat from the truth of our existence in active alcoholism.

We uncover, discover and discard the false self, and find a new peace and serenity in our pursuit of the truth. We continue to watch for the characteristics of our false persona—selfishness, dishonesty, resentment and fear. When these crop up, they create a disturbance within us that requires spiritual psychotherapy for us to regain the emotional balance we find in serenity.

Prayer is the secret ingredient in our restoration to serenity. In solitude we pray and ask God to remove from us the defects of character that threatens our serenity. This is the proper use of prayer for the hopeless alcoholic, whose only hope is the growth and maintenance of a spiritual life.

Selfless prayer is a lifetime practice. When adequately applied, it lifts our thought life above our human perception, to a higher plane in the World of the Spirit. Here, we ascend the Broad Highway and draw ever-nearer to the Sunlight of the Spirit, which burns away within us that which is not of God, and nourishes our spiritual growth to its ultimate destination—a fourth dimension of existence that gets infinitely more wonderful as time passes."

Our blessed brokenness brings healing light to the broken alcoholic

Oldtimer said, "God often uses what He hates to bring to fruition that which He loves. Broken people have a hard time accepting that God would allow them to be broken, or leave them broken, so they pray to be healed from their brokenness. But God uses broken people to do great works in this broken world. It is through our cracks that His light shines into this world and demonstrates His omnipotent grace.

For alcoholics God has a specific purpose for our brokenness. The greater our brokenness, the more Divine Light we can accommodate and project into the lives of others. Nothing is wasted in God's economy. He takes the empty vessel we became, and uses it to carry His grace to those in need. The vessel that carries God's grace is strengthened. The light that shines through our broken cracks to illuminate the lives of others is a healing light that not only heals the recipient of light, but makes the broken vessel transmitting His light whole and complete.

When we fully understand the nature of our brokenness—and God's purpose for it, gratitude becomes our natural state, and we no longer need the world to conform to our desires for us to find happiness and contentment. For instead of being transformed by the world, we are empowered by our Creator to transform the world, one broken alcoholic at a time. For this purpose, our brokenness is the bond that connects us to those most in need of God's grace. As His agents, we bring hope to the broken alcoholic by bearing witness to those we would help of His love, His power, and the omnipotence of His way of life.

Our lives as recovered alcoholics bring depth and weight to the AA message. Thus are we able to bring hope to the hopeless, help to the helpless, and faith to the fearful alcoholic—who is decimated by a cruel taskmaster that takes from them everything, and leaves them broken in so many ways. It is in witnessing the miraculous transformation of the broken alcoholic that our own faith is strengthened, and our gratitude grows exponentially, one redeemed alcoholic at a time."

Alcohol gently embraces us in a death grip

Oldtimer said, "The chains of alcoholism embraced us so gently that by the time we became aware of them, they were too strong to be broken by self-will, self-knowledge, common sense, and reason.

When we arrive in the AA fellowship, we have passed into a state where the most powerful desire to stop drinking is absolutely useless. Pride is the strongest chain in our bondage to self. It ties us to our disease as we sink into the alcoholic pit, and we drown in our sorrows for fear of what others will think of us. This is why, when we finally admit we are an alcoholic, we find that others knew of our condition long before we did. Our pride blinded us, and the fear of being discovered deluded our thinking into ignoring the most obvious facts.

In spite of all the evidence we experienced, we were blind to the reality that we lacked an effective mental defense against the drink idea. If we had an effective defense, we would have never shown up in AA. Common sense, logic, and reason would reveal our weakness for alcohol, and we could use the power of self-will and self-knowledge to stop drinking. Our countless vain attempts to control or moderate our drinking has proven we lack such power. The truth will set us free, but pride often blinds us to the truth. This is why we must rigorously pursue the truth if we are to recover from a mentally defective mind, and end our flight from reality. For it is only through humility that we can properly adjust ourselves to life, rather than trying to fit life to meet our wants and desires.

In order to live life on life's terms, we must first humble ourselves and live life on God's terms. This means we need to quit playing God. When we live and let live, we find that life is a fascinating adventure, and we develop a peaceful coexistence with others. This can only happen if we clean up our side of the street and leave our neighbors side to themselves.

It takes tremendous effort to clear away the wreckage of the past and right the wrongs we have perpetrated upon others. When we are fully engaged in this process, we will not waste time, nor energy, worrying about what others think of us. As we humbly admit our wrongs, commit ourselves to God's way of life, remit the debts we have incurred with others, and carry the message of recovery to the sick and suffering alcoholic, our pride is transformed into a humble respect for our Creator. Through humility, we transmit God's power and become the depth and weight of the AA message.

We have recovered and have been given the power to help others. This is what it means to be an agent of God. This is what it means to be a channel of his peace, love, forgiveness, hope, faith, joy, and light.

To balk is to die

Oldtimer said, "Even when not drinking, we are under the influence of alcohol. Only alcoholics undergo rearrangement of ideas, emotions, and attitudes as a result of consuming alcohol. Everything we think, everything we feel, our whole attitude and outlook upon life centers around alcohol. It told us where to go, who to see, what to do, how to act, and who to be with. This distortion of reality is complete by time we show up in the AA fellowship. We are warned of our fatal condition by those who have recovered. But even with full knowledge of the impending doom we face as a result of alcohol, far too many of us will balk at a change in lifestyle that insures we will live long and sober in this world.

When we balk at the Steps, it is a sure sign that the insanity of alcoholism has a firm grasp on our mind. Unfortunately, the only solution for this lack of willingness is more pain and misery delivered via alcohol. Some people say alcoholics are a weak-willed lot. They know nothing of the tenacity with which we hold onto our ideas, no matter fatal they may be. Only a combination of pain and hope can relieve us of our tenacious grip on our delusional thinking. We thought we had control of our drinking, even as our lack of control was apparent to any sane individual who looked upon the wreckage we heaped upon ourselves.

Driven to AA by the pain of our miserable existence, we found hope in the faces of others who had once suffered as we did, but now have the look of victory in their eyes. They have laughter in their voice that drowns out the pain of a dreary existence in the alcoholic pit. They offered us evidence that no matter how far we had slid down into the alcoholic pit, our chance for a new way of life was ours, so long as we let go of our old ideas and accepted **G**ood **O**rderly **D**irections. For once, we were presented with a bargain that offered us far more than we deserved. It was ours for the taking if we only let go of our prejudice toward God, and allowed Him to work in our life.

We found that God can do for you only what you allow Him to do through you. So long as we live His way of life and carry the message of recovery to others, we will recover from a hopeless state of mind and body."

Wisdom begins with freedom from fear

Oldtimer said, "Until we turn our will and our lives over to the care of God, our lives remain unmanageable and we float from crisis to crisis, in a sober state of mind. This isn't the insanity of the first drink, but the insanity of bondage to self. All action is preceded by thought, and it is our twisted ideas, emotions, and attitudes that create the dysfunction and drama in our lives. So long as we rely on our own will, we do the same thing over and over again, with the expectation of a different results. If we want different results, we must do something we have never done before.

When we follow **G**ood **O**rderly **D**irections, we break the vicious cycle of self-destruction that began with our first drink and continues to progress in our sobriety, as long as we continue to make decisions based on self. Self-seeking fear drives us into a delusional state of mind where **F**alse **E**vidence **A**ppears **R**eal.

At the end of our alcoholic careers, alcohol twisted our mind to the point that we could not determine the true from the false about alcohol. This delusional dynamic spreads to every facet of our life. Self-reliance fails us because it is rooted in the lie that we could wrest satisfaction and happiness out of this world, if we only managed well. This is our agnostic nature that fears God and will not surrender to His way of life. From this nature stems all manner of delusions.

Fear of God is said to be the beginning of wisdom. Perhaps this is true for believers who do not suffer from a hopeless state of mind and body. Their survival in this world isn't dependent upon a dire need for a spiritual experience. For alcoholics, wisdom comes from a through examination of our past mistakes, and a sincere desire to set right the wrongs we have committed. When we accept the role God has assigned, and allow Him to manage our lives, we are no longer driven by a self-centered fear that drives the self-delusion, self-seeking, and self-pity that are the main characteristics of our agnostic nature. When we rigorously pursue the truth, we draw near God, and as a result, our fears fall from us.

Free from this debilitating malady, we begin to have a transformative spiritual experience, and lose our fear of today, tomorrow, or the hereafter. As a result, our spiritual channel is clear of the wreckage of the past, and we intuitively know how to handle situations which used to baffle us. We are then in much less danger of excitement, fear, anger worry, self-pity, or foolish decisions. No longer are we a slave to our emotional nature, or prey to misery and depression. Our lives become manageable when we lose our fear of God, fire the insane manager, and allow God to order our steps.

In this new relationship with our Creator, we sacrifice our delusional self-centered fear in exchange for the keys to the Great Reality within, and find much of Heaven as we trudge along the road to our happy destiny."

Selfishness, self-seeking is the root of our sex problems

Oldtimer said, "Lust is another form of self-seeking. As alcoholics, it was a way of life. We lusted mightily for the drink. The pleasure it brought us was intoxicating. So, too, is our experience with sex. The pleasure it brings us is overwhelming and has the ability to rearrange our ideas, emotions, and attitudes the same way alcohol does. Dealing with pleasure of any sort requires discipline if we are to grow a life based on spiritual principles.

Alcoholics are easily addicted to pleasure. If it taste good, smells good, feels good, or makes us feel good, we are liable to rearrange our priorities to acquire as much as we can, as often as we can. So it is with sex. Our sex powers are God-given, but alcoholics often misuse this gift.

Many draw their identity from it. For some, it is a power tool that is used to build, or even destroy. Some use it as a mask to hide their vulnerability. But when given as an expression of love, and received as such, it's effects can be cathartic.

For those who find it problematic, the key lies in treating it like any other problem in recovery. Through the use of inventory, prayer, and meditation we find relief from the selfishness that is at the center of our dysfunction. In our self-centeredness, we think of ourselves first and only, wringing from sex our pleasures, while ignoring our impact on others.

Alcoholics are lover of things and users of people. We must discipline ourselves to be considerate of others and hard on ourselves if we are to balance the pleasure of sex with the spiritual principles that guide us in our new way of life. In doing so, we acknowledge that our Creator is bigger than the problems we create with our sexual pursuit, and the solution to our sex problems lies in His will for us.

Service is the secret. If sex is very troublesome we throw ourselves harder into helping others. This experience with selflessness soon manifests in our sex life. For love is service, and when we go into a relationship seeking to give rather than receive, we find that we are in concert with spiritual principles, and we nourish our spiritual growth through our sex life.

Sex is usually the last surrender we make to God. His solution always involves some form of discipline and alcoholics and addicts are an undisciplined lot known for placing pleasure over principles. But when we follow God's guidance, He provides what we need in all of our affairs, and we live a life of promise and purpose."

Let it be written. Let it be spoken. Let it be done

Oldtimer said, "The spiritual life is not a theory. We have to live it if we expect to live long and happily in this world. As God's people, we live with purpose and passion. We must put our knees to the ground and partake in selfless prayer and meditation, seeking only knowledge of God's will for us and the power to carry it out. We must cast aside our alcoholic sense of justice by casting aside self-seeking, and, instead, seek to balance the scales of justice by making amends to those we have harmed, and offering forgiveness to those who have harmed us. We must remain cognizant of our shortcomings by taking the high road in pursuit for the perfect spiritual ideals, rather than our lower, base instincts for sex, society and security.

It is in pursuing these perfect spiritual ideals that the nature of our defects of character are revealed. We must remain at the ready to have God remove these defects of character, and practice daily the rigors of unselfishness, love, purity and honesty.

When we go to meetings we find a safe harbor to practice these principles, and through this practice comes a change in our worldly behavior. We must continue to take personal inventory and share our findings with a close-mouthed, understanding friend.

"Let it be written, let it be spoken, let it be done," is our methodology for spiritual growth. We admit our wrongs to God for forgiveness. We admit our wrongs to ourselves for acceptance. We admit our wrongs to others for humility. And in doing so, we begin to feel the nearness of our Creator, and become willing to do His will in all of our affairs. Each day becomes a day we carry the vision of God's will into all of our affairs. Keeping our sobriety first will insure that it will last.

When recovery is foremost in our priorities, it drives our choices and leads us to take actions that strengthen our relationship with our Creator. Some days we may be sicker than others, but this is only in proportion to our willingness to reveal our secrets. Through the application of the kit of spiritual tools to our lives, inventory transforms into confession, which transforms into a change in outlook and reaction to the world about us. When we apply these tools to all of our affairs, all of the time, we take up residence in the World of the Spirit and fit ourselves for maximum service to God and our fellow man."

Step Six is willingness to apply Step Ten to our lives

Oldtimer said, "Step Six and Seven are essential to our spiritual practice in Step Ten. In Step Six, our new relationship with pain drives our willingness to change. In Step Seven, we exchange the guilt and shame that lies on the axis of our perception of good and bad or right and wrong, and operate on the axis of true and false." For, by now, we understand that we weren't bad people, but sick people doing our best with the devastation alcohol inflicted upon us.

Now we bring forth a Teachable Spirit within us that helps us correct our mistakes. In this state, we are better aligned with the spiritual world, and we work to remove the mistakes in perception that feed the ego, and instead act upon the change in behavior that will reinforce the Spirit. We become much more sensitive to our motives rooted in selfishness, dishonesty, resentment, and fear, and become willing to release them and embrace God's will instead.

As this change occurs, our prayers for relief from the bondage of self are much more effective, and we undergo spiritual growth that alters our perception and reaction to life. The Eternal Spirit within unites with our mind, and we perceive eternity itself, as well as our place in it. This alters our value system, and we invest more in that which is eternal—the World of the Spirit-and less in that which is limited-the material world, in which the ego thrives.

It is our pursuit of material goals that cause us to Ease God Out. In Steps Six and Seven, we accept our role as agents for God, and our motivations change, as do our choices, perceptions, and actions. Now, we pursue spiritual goals, and our past harms to others become the stairway on which we ascend, amends by amends, to a new life in the fourth dimension of existence."

Pride leaves us enslaved to our defects of character

Oldtimer said, "Our defects of character represent the links in the chain that binds us to our old ideas, emotions, and attitudes. Pride, anger, greed, gluttony, envy, lust, and sloth served us well in our alcoholic life. Acting out on them seemed right, justified, and normal. They enabled to survive the rigors of a fatal malady that took everything from us, and left us with nothing.

Pride leads the procession. It justifies every other shortcoming of our behavior that makes our life unmanageable. Pride tells us we are better than others, and we become angry when they don't recognize it. Even worse, anger from past experiences pile on top of our anger in the present, and manifests into a resentment that threatens to destroy us.

Greed and gluttony are projections of selfishness driven by pride which tells us that our superiority qualifies us for more than we deserve. In our pride-driven superiority, we covet our neighbor's possessions simply because we feel we deserve them. We believe we need not work for our achievements. Our superior status makes all that we see our birth right. We want what we want, when we want it, and pride inflames our passions beyond reason until we obsess over that which has been denied us. This lustful approach to life leads us into inconsiderate habits that destroy sweet relationships and leaves many homes in dysfunction.

Sloth is the end result of pride. We feel we deserve everything and it should be given us, even when we don't work for it. Ultimately, pride leads us back to the drink. We cannot accept that we were defeated by alcohol, so we re-enter a losing battle against the bottle that has ended the life of many prideful alcoholics. It is only when alcohol humbles us, and we accept defeat, that we start to let loose of our deadly pride and grow into right relations with our Creator and our fellow man.

In the humiliation of the First Step, we accept the truth of our relationship with alcohol. In the humility of the remaining Steps, we accept a newfound relationship with God. He is the Father, and we are His children, whom he blesses with unmerited favor and grace. This grace brings us freedom from the bondage of self, and restores our defects of character into virtuous behaviors that allow us to rebuild our lives. We humbly restore what we destroyed with our pride, and enter a way of life that gets infinitely more wonderful as time passes."

Broken trust calls for an amends

Oldtimer said, "Saying I am sorry is sufficient when a mistake has been made. But amends is necessary when we have broken a trust.

Our amends list reveals that we are weapons of mass destruction, executed one relationship at a time. We have left a trail of broken bonds that were built on mutual trust because we thought only of ourselves and stepped on the toes of our fellow man. Our self-centered nature is the tool of destruction that brought physical, financial, emotional, and spiritual harm to those who entered our life.

A business which takes no inventory usually goes broke, and when we came to AA, we were broken. We were full of self-loathing which we passed on to others. As a result, sweet relationships are dead, and homes have been left in chaos and confusion as we transmitted our disease to those in our orbit. Through inventory, we made a list of what we have broken, and are prepared to repair the damage done in the past.

Hurt people hurt people. As alcoholics we magnified our pain and passed it on to others because we failed to take an honest stock of the impact our actions had on others. Now, we endeavor to determine when we made an honest mistake, versus when we have broken the trust people placed in us. In nine cases out of ten, we have repeatedly broken trust with our actions, which resulted in harms to others. Only through amends (change) is it even remotely possible to regain the trust of our loved ones. We treated their trust as we did an empty shot glass that no longer provided us with what we wanted. We sacrificed them to our lower power, that we might continue to pursue the drink that was destroying our lives.

Only under God's guidance, through honest actions, and a sincere desire to clean up the wreckage of the past, can we alcoholics repair the damage we have done with our efforts to run the show ourselves!"

Making amends is a power move

Oldtimer said, "The amends process is a power move for the alcoholic. We are powerless over alcohol. This weakness makes us uniquely situated to bring forth God's power by humbly admitting our wrongs and making amends for them.

The first part of our amends comes in the Fourth Step, when we put out of our minds the wrongs of others, and become willing to set right our wrongs. We can't do a proper Fourth Step without accepting that purpose and keeping forgiveness in the forefront of our minds.

The second part of our amends is revealed in the Resentment Prayer when we ask how we can be helpful to the people that harmed us, and ask for God's will to guide us in correcting the error of our ways. The third part is when we stand face to face with those we have harmed, admit our wrongs, and allow them to set the terms of restitution for our amends. The fourth part is a change in our behavior going forward. If we do not change the offending behavior, and continue to act out on them, our amends prove insufficient, and this paves the way back to the bottle.

The opportunity to engage in the old behavior will present itself on occasion. This is when the rubber meets the road, and we must choose between God's will and our will. As we continue to clean our side of the street, we must take care that we don't litter it with a repeat of our old behavior, in a new circumstance. Once we clean our side of street, we walk in the corridor of Infinite Power and Infinite Love. The fear, regret, remorse, guilt, and shame that blocked us from God's power falls before us as we humble ourselves, forgive our trespassers, and make the necessary amends. In this way do we accept God's forgiveness for ourselves and find His love, power, and grace with every amends we make."

Easing God Out leads to complacency

Oldtimer said, "The alcoholic that comes into AA on day one will drink again. For when we come into the rooms of recovery, we bring with us the seeds of our destruction.

The AA solution to alcoholism is not fighting the drink one day at a time. This is a fight that the alcoholic has consistently lost. If we are to win our battle against alcohol, we must win it on the battleground of the mind. We cannot win this battle in solitary conflict. The same sick mind that created the problem cannot solve the problem it created. Solitary combat against an opponent we are powerless against can have only one result-failure! Thus do so many alcoholics return to the bottle after a period of self-imposed sobriety.

The experience of millions of alcoholics who have recovered has shown that we must surrender to win the battle against the bottle. We must surrender from alcohol. For it has proven to be a destructive power greater than ourselves.

We must surrender to God, for He is the One who has all Power-a power we access by living His way of life.

This is a simple task, but it is the most difficult one we will ever undertake. In surrendering to God, we encounter the alcoholic ego, which stands in direct opposition to the **G**ood **O**rderly **D**irections that is our salvation. The ego is the author of chaos in the life of the alcoholic. When we **E**ase **G**od **O**ut, we lose interest in the work that is necessary to recover from a hopeless state of mind and body. We place our focus on gratifying our instincts for sex, society and security and the pleasure they offer. Selfishness, dishonesty, resentment, and fear are agents of the ego that provide us great physical pleasures. A pleasure that cloaks an evil that leads us back to the bottle. This is our deal with the devil that is the alcoholic ego. We can feel good even as we destroy our lives.

God offers us rest from the restless, irritable state of discontentment that the ego creates in our soul. By removing the agents of the ego from our life, and maintaining conscious contact with God, His power flows into us and we are no longer transformed by the world, but by the spirituality of the Steps. Through the Steps, we experience a psychic change. We are relieved of our obsession to drink, released from the bondage to the ego, and become resistant to the temptations of the world. So long as we stay close to our Creator and perform His work well, our behavior becomes a demonstration of God's omnipotence, which we demonstrate to others who seek escape from alcoholism."

While we are conscious we need contact with God

Oldtimer said, "Sought through prayer and meditation to improve our conscious contact with God, as we understood Him." While we are conscious, we need to contact God and improve upon the relationship we started with our Third Step decision.

In Step Three, we turn our will (thoughts) and our life (actions) over to the care and direction of God. The emphasis of this Step is selfless prayer and service to others. We pray for freedom from the bondage of self. Our old ideas, emotions, and attitudes, rooted in self-centeredness, dominate our mind and comprise the alcoholic thinking that inevitably leads back to alcoholic drinking. Relapse begins long before we begin drinking. It begins with our thinking.

Selfish thoughts, dishonest thoughts, resentful thoughts, and fearful thoughts clog our communication channel with God. Our bondage to these thoughts are so great that we place them before God's will. Thus are we denied access to

His power, and remain powerless over alcohol. Thus is our life made unmanageable with unsound and insane ideas. Thus do we return to the way of death found in the bottle.

Our alcoholic mind serves us not. It is out to get us. No matter how intelligent we may appear, in reality, we are outright mental detectives with suicidal tendencies that we express one drink at a time. When this is understood in its entirety, we are more likely to surrender to God's way of life without reservation. This surrender is incomplete without prayer and meditation. Prayer is talking to God. Meditation is listening for God's response. Prayer, when properly applied, increases our effectiveness in communicating with God, and understanding His will for us. When we pray the resentment prayer we silence the thunderstorm of recycled anger that holds our attention. When we pray the fear prayer False Evidence Appearing Real falls away and the truth comes to us in the stillness of our mind.

The opposite of fear is faith, and faith means courage. It takes a great deal of courage to seek the stillness of mind when our human instincts rebel at such a notion and demand immediate action to satisfy them. We must train our mind to accept peace, and this requires a steady practice of meditation.

Meditation doesn't mean we control our thoughts; it means we no longer let our thoughts control us. Meditation makes apparent our mind's incessant attempt to communicate with us. It is the noise that takes place whenever we try to silence our mind. This is the stream of consciousness of which we have only been vaguely aware. Repeated practice at meditation brings release from its control, and what used to be the occasional hunch, gradually becomes a part of our working mind. In the stillness of the mind, our sixth sense is awakened, and we are better able to intuitively understand God's will for us. We have fit ourselves for maximum service to our Creator and His creation."

Completely giving ourselves to a simple solution

Oldtimer said, "We have an illness that takes no time off. Alcoholism is at work twenty-four

hours a day, seven days a week, and three-hundred sixty-five days a year. It doesn't take holidays off, and so long as we are thinking, it is ever-present. Even when we recover from the obsession, it speaks to us in more subtle tones to keep us from doing what we need to do to stay recovered. Anytime we balk at anything the Steps requires, we are handing our illness firm footing in our mind, from which it can launch another relapse.

Are we applying inventory to our life on a daily basis? Are we practicing prayer and meditation? Are we carrying the AA message to the sick and suffering alcoholic? Are we practicing the principles of the AA program in all of our affairs?

Only when we answer these questions in the affirmative can we say that we have an effective spiritual defense against the first drink. We do recover from alcoholism, but this is a conditional state, not a permanent condition. We can recover from a gun shot wound, but it doesn't mean we can't get shot again. So it is with recovery from alcoholism. One shot, and we're all shot.

It is easy to let up on our spiritual program of action, and rest on our laurels. Steps Ten, Eleven, and Twelve are the disciplines of recovery. Undisciplined people are easily addicted to pleasure, but we have learned from our experience with alcohol that evil often comes cloaked in pleasure. The key to long-term sobriety is the **G**ood **O**rderly **D**iscipline applied to the **G**ood **O**rderly **D**irections that Alcoholics Anonymous offers as a solution to our spiritual malady.

In the word spiritual, we find the word ritual. So long as we practice this ritual that has been proven to work, we maintain a happy, contented sobriety. As long as we trust God, clean house, love God, and help others, we help ourselves to the gift of His abundant grace. This ritual has been tried, tested, and found true in the lives of millions of alcoholics who recovered from a hopeless state of mind and body.

Due to the relentless nature of alcoholism, we must completely give ourselves to this simple program if we expect to live long and happily in this life. And this means a lifetime of spiritual development. When we do so, we come to know a new happiness, and new freedom, in a way of life where the quantity of our problems decreases, and the quality of our solution increases."

Controlled drinking is a delusional form of alcoholic drinking

Oldtimer said, "When an alcoholic tries to control their drinking, they have already gone beyond the point of no return and have lost control of their drinking. The act of controlling one's drinking is an admission that the one has lost control, and therefore, needs to take action to control it. This is, in fact, an admission that the alcoholic is powerless over alcohol because only alcoholics drink to the point where they need to control their drinking.

Temperate drinkers, or even hard drinkers, simply decide to stop or moderate, and are able to follow through with it. We of the alcoholic persuasion all have had countless vain attempts to control our drinking, but inevitably the truth came crashing through in the form of a crisis that followed yet another alcoholic spree. In spite of our powers of self-delusion, the truth came to us, and we could no longer evade or postpone our inevitable demise into alcoholic oblivion.

Trying to control a drinking habit is often the last desperate act before the final fatality of alcoholism takes over. Every alcoholic takes their last drink. It either takes us to the grave, or brings us to AA with a sense of desperation that drives our commitment to the Twelve Steps.

Faith without works is dead, and willingness without action is fantasy. We find that faith alone was insufficient to overcome a maddening obsession for alcohol, and our shallow willingness to change amounts to nothing more than another good intention that paves our way to the alcoholic pit. Unless we take the actions prescribed by AA, our days, like the Steps, are numbered. We are beyond human aid, and only through the aid of a power greater than ourselves can we master alcohol and regain control of our lives.

In recovery, we don't exert willingness toward controlling our drinking, but toward surrendering our will and life to God. And with each day we successfully surrender to the **G**ood **O**rderly **D**irections AA offers, do we find ourselves easily able to control our desire for alcohol. By placing our focus on the Steps, the problem of the obsession is removed and we will rarely give thought to drinking. If we do, we recoil from it as from a hot flame.

This is the great news AA carries to every alcoholic who has lost control of their drinking. Every alcoholic has one last drink in them. In AA we live to talk about it."

Consuming our daily bread is a matter of willingness

Oldtimer said, "A sober day on self-will is a relapse waiting to happen. The Alcoholics Anonymous solution to alcoholism is change. We say relapse happens long before we pick up a drink. It actually starts when we refuse to pick up the kit of spiritual tools that are designed to grow and maintain a spiritual life.

We can't think our way out of a drink, but we can act our way out of thinking a drink is a good idea. The problem of the alcoholic centers in the mind. We can change our playmates, playgrounds, and playthings all we wish, but unless we experience an entire psychic change our old playmates, playgrounds, and playthings will return to our lives as soon as we pick up a drink.

Every day is a day we must live life on a spiritual basis, or run the risk of another bout of terror, bewilderment, frustration, and despair delivered to us with the next drink. If we only exchange meetings for bars, sober friends for drunk friends and coffee for alcohol, we have done nothing to effectively treat our mental illness known as alcoholism. And as long as we have an alcoholic mind, we are likely to drink once again. This has been proven by millions of alcoholics over the decades of AA's existence. Those who cannot, or will not, completely give themselves to the simple program of recovery that AA offers, fall prey to relapse time and time again until they meet their ultimate, unfortunate demise.

God has prepared for us a spiritual buffet of His unlimited grace, yet some of us show up and pick over a few olives because we don't want to weigh our plates down too much. Or we ignore the spiritual nourishment offered, for fear of the positive change it will bring to our life. Unfortunately, many alcoholics find comfort in the misery that is familiar to them, and choose to stay in it, rather than face the discomfort of change. God will not force feed His grace to us. Nor does He withdraw it from us when we refuse to accept it. He gives us each day our daily bread, but we must pickup our kit of spiritual tools and bake the bread we desire. Only we hold the key of willingness to participate in the celestial buffet of God's grace that is the program of Alcoholics Anonymous."

The Third Step is an offer God can't refuse

Oldtimer said. "God, I offer myself to Thee to build with me and do with me as Thou will."

In this prayer we are entering a partnership with God to reconstruct our lives with Him at the center. This is an offer God will not refuse. No matter how far down the well of inequity we have fallen, God offers us redemption and another chance at abundant life. Even though we are full of self-loathing for ourselves, God has always radiated His unlimited love upon us. He loved us when we were at our worse, because He knew it was the best we could do under the circumstances we were dealt.

It is only after we shed the delusions of self that we come to realize God was loving us when we could not love ourselves. With our Third Step decision, we are now on God's side in our battle against the bottle. It is a battle we let Him fight while we fit ourselves to serve as His agents.

We begin construction of the arch through which we walk free of our bondage to alcohol by seeking freedom from bondage to self—our old ideas, emotions, and attitudes that were marinated in alcohol. We cannot serve two masters, and self constantly exerts it's will upon us by drawing on our instincts for sex, society, and security. When we choose to pursue the fool's gold they offer, we find ourselves restless, irritable, and discontented, and thoughts of the ease and comfort of the first drink come on strongly.

We have no effective mental defense against this obsession for drink. Alcohol has in its employ many agents that work within us. Our only defense comes from a power that rest in our Divine Consciousness. When we choose to serve God, we draw upon the power of our Divine Consciousness to do for us what we cannot do for ourselves—determine the true from the false. Our choice to serve God is a choice to pursue the truth about who we are and Whose we are. We have served many false gods and placed them before our Creator. We did their bidding, and it led us to ruin. Fortunately, we have a God who serves us and offers us redemption, no matter how many times we have fallen.

When we surrender our will and life to Him, He does not make the terms of surrender to difficult. We will always receive more than we give in recovery. We are not asked to mindlessly follow Him, nor are we required to take a blind leap of faith into the unknown. The AA fellowship gives us ample evidence of the wonders of His work with alcoholics who bear witness to His love, His power, and His way of life.

We still live in the age of miracles. So long as we live up to our commitment in the Third Step, and perform the work necessary to bring about freedom from the bondage of self, we become miracles in the making with every surrender we make and every Step we take."

Now about sex and shame

Oldtimer said, "Our sexual misconduct brings more shame into our lives than any other human endeavor. Shame is a thick cloud that will block us from the Sunlight of the Spirit, which we need to grow into the image of our Creator.

When we serve God, we turn our libido, and its pleasures, over to His care, and the **G**ood **O**rderly **D**irections the AA program provides. In this area of life, many of us need an overhauling. When a mechanic overhauls a car engine, they don't jump in and work on a hot engine. They first let it cool down before they begin their work. So it is with us.

Alcohol has heightened our sensory perception and we have become hyper-sexual individuals. We see the world through our carnal lens and project our pursuit of pleasure into the sex arena once we are denied the intoxicating effects of alcohol. In recovery, we have to perform the delicate balance of disciplining our sexual instinct to conform to our newfound spiritual life. We ask God to mold our sex ideals, and help us to live up to them. For some of us, this may mean a period of abstinence. Like alcohol, we need to detox from the intoxicating effects of our sexual appetite.

For others, who have long suffered under past sexual abuse, the work goes much deeper. We don't despise or loath our sexuality, nor do we treat it lightly or selfishly. We simply treat sex as we would any other problem. Through the discipline of inventory, we develop an amends list for our own selfish, sexual misconduct. We uncover and discover the harm we have inflicted upon others with our drive for sexual gratification. We identify our defects of character that led to the abuse and ask God to remove them.

Were we dishonest when we spoke words of love that covered a lustful motive? Was our thinking inconsiderate? Were we thinking only of what we could get out of the affair? Are we willing to make these matters right? For if we fail to right our wrongs, and continue to harm others we are sure to drink.

If we, ourselves, have been harmed by another's sexual misconduct, forgiveness is essential if we desire freedom from the bondage of abuse that keeps us locked in the cycle of shame and despair. Without forgiveness we become our own jailer, and the emotional abuse we heap upon ourselves is far more damaging than the original abuse. Whatever the case may be in our dysfunctional sex life, we ask in prayer and meditation what we should do in each specific matter.

As we apply Good Orderly Discipline to our sex life, we are transformed by the Spirit into the loving image of our Creator. And as we stay under His guidance, the quality of those we attract, and are attracted to, will change into more fulfilling intimate relationships. Eventually, our attraction is on the plane of the Spirit, and we form whole and healthy relationships that help us to continue to grow spiritually and increase our servitude to the One Master who has all power."

The double life of the alcoholic ends at Step Five

Oldtimer said, "If you tell the truth, you never have to remember it. It takes a great deal of energy to live the lie that is the alcoholic life. More than most people, we live a double life—full of secrets we keep hidden from the world. These secrets keep us sick until we ultimately die from them. We cannot continue to live our double life if we expect to live long and happily in God's world. The truth will set us free when we expose our secrets, and will keep us bound to shame if we don't.

In our double life we have a public persona that we project to the world, and then there is the private inner life with all the secrets we keep hidden from the world for fear of what others will think of us. We may escape public shame when we keep our secrets, but we live in a private Hell for the shame we have toward ourselves. This makes life on life's terms a living hell that requires more alcohol to escape the torture of our twisted alcoholic mind. This is why it is important for an alcoholic to experience the depth of sharing that occurs in the Fifth Step. This is necessary to combat the falsehoods the ego has been feeding us about the need to keep our innermost thoughts secret. This is how the ego keeps us sick, and ultimately, leads us back to the bottle so we can complete the self-destruction we interrupted when we put the bottle down.

The truth shared with a closed-mouth, understanding friend frees us from the bondage of shame and ushers in a sense of peace and serenity which we have never felt. After the initial experience with the Fifth Step, the newcomer begins to shares much deeper, and more honestly in the rooms. They willingly open up about their secrets because of the freedom they experienced in their Fifth Step, and they want to hold on to that sense of release and comfort that comes when we admit to God, ourselves, and another human being the exact nature of our wrongs. In doing so, they become a demonstration of the omnipotence of God and His infinite capacity for mercy, love, and forgiveness. The forgiveness, humility, and acceptance found in our original confession thus becomes the new normal we seek to maintain in our spiritual walk with the Creator of the Universe."

Our mental attitude determines our spiritual altitude

Oldtimer said, "Step Six and Seven are attitude adjustments essential to our spiritual progress in recovery. In Step Six, we adopt a willingness to change. Here spiritual progress is the goal. Pain is the taproot of our spiritual growth because we refuse to let go of some of our defects of character and let God take us to better things. Instead, we hang on to them until the pain of humiliation crushes the wall of pride that acts as a barrier to God's will. Thus do we adopt a new attitude toward pain. And instead of avoiding it, we accept pain as a signpost that redirects us on to a higher road.

If we haven't the willingness to change, we simply pray for the willingness we lack. And when the pain of staying the same becomes greater than the pain of changing, we finally become willing to change.

In Step Seven we exchange the guilt and shame that lies on the axis of our perception of good and bad, or right and wrong, and bring forth a Teachable Spirit within that helps us correct our mistakes. In this state, we are better aligned with the spiritual world, and work to remove the mistakes in perception that feed the ego, and accept the change in behavior that will reinforce the Spirit. As a result, we become much more sensitive to our selfishness, dishonesty, resentment, and fear, and become more willing to release them and embrace God's will instead. As this change occurs, our prayers for relief from the bondage of self are much more effective, and we undergo a spiritual growth spurt that alters our perception and reaction to life.

The Eternal Spirit within unites with our mind, and we perceive eternity itself, as well as our place in it. This alters our value system, and we invest more in that which is eternal—the World of the Spirit, and less in that which is limited—the material world in which the ego thrives. It is our pursuit of material goals that caused us to Ease God Out.

In Steps Six and Seven we commit ourselves to service, and accept our role as agents for God. And when we accept the role He assigns, we are able to match calamity with serenity. God doesn't call the qualified to His service, but qualifies those who answer His call. As His agents, our motivations change, as does our choices, perceptions, and actions. Now, our past harms to others become the stairway we ascend, amends by amends, to achieve a new life in the fourth dimension, and a happy, joyous and free existence in this world."

Our instincts run on impulse power

Oldtimer said, "Alcoholics are impulsive people. Our obsession for alcohol programmed us to feel, act, and then think. This maladjustment to life left us in a self-centered state where immediate gratification became the norm. We want what we want, when we want it, and the sooner the better. In our self-seeking pursuits, we were hard on others and considerate only of ourselves. This impulsivity gave rise to the emotional deformities that fed our obsession for alcohol.

When we are entirely ready to have God remove our defects of character, we become willing to participate in our transformation, and continue to watch for selfishness, dishonesty, resentment and fear. These bedevilments spring forth from our instincts for sex, society, and security. When we respond to these impulses, we create chaos and confusion in the lives of others, and they then project it back into our lives. We step on their toes, and then they retaliate. Our response is either resentment or self-pity. Both lead us back to the bottle. Only the truth can set us free from this cycle of death, destruction, and ruin.

"Know thyself, and to thine own self be true," may well be our rallying cry to sanity. We can no longer fool ourselves about values. Alcoholics are a mystery wrapped in an enigma. We have character defects that work against us, and we have character assets that we work against. We may be kind, considerate, modest, and self-sacrificing, but we use our good qualities for illicit means.

If we are to survive both our defects and assets, we must change our purpose. For in purpose lies power. When we change our purpose, it changes our thoughts. When we change our thoughts, it changes our choices. When we change our choices, it changes our actions. When we change our actions, it changes our life. Therefore, we turn our will and our life over to God, good and bad, and put ourselves fully into His service.

When God's purpose becomes our purpose, our motives change, and we are no longer transformed by the world, but by the quickening of the Spirit. We become His agents, and rest in His abundance with assurance that His grace is sufficient."

Our amends list reflects a new perspective on the world about us

Oldtimer said, "Alcoholics are childish, emotionally sensitive and grandiose. We are maladjusted to life, mentally defectives, and in full flight from reality. In this state, we are easily offended. So much so that our feelings are hurt when someone simply doesn't do what we expected them to do. Even when they don't know what it is we want, we are hurt because they failed to read our mind. When this occurs, it feels like they are doing something to us, when in fact, they are doing something for themselves.

These uncomfortable feelings are real to us, but they do not reflect reality. To avoid this resentment trap, we must learn how to handle the BAR principle. In our emotionally sensitive state betrayal, abandonment and rejection is inflicted upon us constantly, and our learned pattern of behavior is to drink over this pain. For these bedevilments, acceptance is the answer.

As alcoholics trying to live a spiritual life, we must accept our transgressors as sick people. They, like us, are spiritually sick. This brings balance to the relationship and allows room for forgiveness to rise from the spiritual realm to our consciousness, where it can be most effective.

Forgiveness is not a one time act. It is an ongoing process that brings healing to fractured relationships. It needs to become a way of life for the alcoholic. If our hope is permanent recovery, we must be prepared to look at life from an entirely different angle. This is apparent with our amends list. It is full of people who have harmed us, and that we need to forgive before we begin our amends.

When we complain about ourselves, or others, we lack acceptance and have been offended on the emotional level. This is where we must bring the spiritual healing that amends provide. The world and its people are quite often wrong, and often quite wrong. This is why a great master told his followers to turn the other cheek and forgive seven times seventy. We need to eat, sleep and breathe forgiveness because there will always be a time someone in the world will continue to betray us, abandon us and reject us.

Hurt people hurt people, and it benefits the alcoholic greatly to consider what happened to their transgressors in their human experience that brought on the pain they have passed along to us. Ultimately, the answer is their ego mind. When you Ease God Out, you can inflict untold harm upon others. We have done this, and should be able to recognize the same behavior in others. If we got it, we can spot it. We knew not our spiritual nature, and brought great harm to others. So it is with others.

Now, as agents for God, we seek forgiveness by offering forgiveness, and bring balance to God's world by living His way of life. When we live with God at the center of our being, we will harm no one. We seek only to be helpful. Therefore, when we accept others as spiritually sick people, and demonstrate the power of forgiveness, we are operating at the maximum level of service we can perform for God, the world, and our transgressors."

A change in behavior requires courage that comes from God

Oldtimer said, "Amends means change. True amends involves a change in our nature so profound that the alcoholic cannot fathom the thought of repeating the action for which they have made amends. This change in personality is synonymous with the psychic change that occurs as a result of a spiritual awakening. We are no longer the same alcoholic who came into AA on day one.

When we change the nature of our being, we change the nature of our relationships. Including our relationship with alcohol. By taking the lead in making the necessary amends, we reflect a newfound courage that comes as a result of our newfound faith in God—a faith reflected in the Steps we take to stay sober.

Faith means courage, and the actions taken in Steps Eight and Nine are a far cry from the cowardly personality that tried to keep our wrongs hidden. In doing so, we only fueled our obsession to drink. To make amends is to bring balance to the relationship by placing the center of power in the hands of those we have harmed. We have no need for this earthly power, for we now have the power of God supporting us. Therefore, we allow our victims to tell us how deeply we have hurt them, for they need to do so in order to affect the healing process. We allow them to set the terms for restitution, and do our level best to live up to them so that we might be restored to sanity and find healing as well.

When we amend the nature of our character, we amend the nature of our relationships, This change in our nature is rooted in Steps Six and Seven where we accepted our defective nature and became willing to have God remove the defects of character responsible for our offensive behavior. Steps Eight and Nine are where the changes brought about in Steps Six and Seven are expressed in the lives of those we have harmed. Going forward with our amends reflects the courage that comes from the trust we have placed in God.

Where God guides He provides. And when we rely upon Him, we are endowed with the power we need to make our amends and to live up to them."

Old behavior is our disease with God's will

Oldtimer said, "We are not cured of alcoholism. We must outgrow it everyday by removing its source of nutrition. Selfishness, dishonesty, resentment, and fear are fertilizer for the thinking disease that is alcoholism. It is a mental illness rooted in stinking thinking, which manifests into the stinking drinking that sends us on another ruinous alcoholic spree. We think ourselves into a drink, and then drink ourselves into a grave. Therefore, it could be said that alcoholics think themselves to death.

All action is preceded by thought. Whenever we find ourselves acting out with old behavior, it is time to take inventory of our thought processes. Selfishness, dishonesty resentment and fear produce thoughts that return us to our alcoholic behavior. We then rationalize, justify, and minimize the behavior by blaming others for initiating our response to their behavior. This is why we must make a habit of putting out of our minds the wrongs of others. This requires a constant attitude of forgiveness. It is easier to maintain this attitude when we realize that hurt people hurt people, and whatever harm they brought to us was a reflection of a harm done unto them. They weren't necessarily doing something to us. They were doing something for themselves. So we accept the offending party as spiritually sick, and place our focus on our spiritual dis-ease.

Selfishness, dishonesty, resentment and fear are evidence of our dis-ease with God's will. Thus does vengeance, not forgiveness, become our response to those who wronged us. Therefore, we ask God to take away the defect of character that led to our alcoholic behavior, and direct our attention to the right thought or right action needed to bring our relationship with our Creator back into balance. When the dis-ease is healed, we can easily forgive those who trespassed against us, and find healing in the forgiveness we offer our enemy. Thus is our enemy transformed into a teacher who brought us a lesson of redemption born of forgiveness."

The power of prayer flows through a clear channel

Oldtimer said, "Our success in recovery is directly proportional to our reliance upon prayer and meditation. There is power in prayer. The greater our use of prayer, the greater the power flows into our lives, and the greater our chances of maintaining our recovery from a hopeless state of mind and body.

We shouldn't be shy on this matter of prayer. It has been effectively used by many before us since the dawn of time. When we pray for knowledge of God's will for us, prayer becomes the question, and mediation becomes the answer. We must employ both to recover. Even when we are tasked with making amends to those we harmed, we turn to God and ask how we can right the wrongs we have inflicted upon others. We then listen in meditation. The right answer will come if we want it. In fact, it comes even if we do not want it. No prayer goes unanswered. However, alcoholics will ignore the answer if it does not fit their level of willingness.

We must be willing to go to any lengths for victory over alcohol, and only God knows what is required.

In Step Seven, we renew our Third Step commitment with increased fervor, for now we are fully aware of the seriousness of our condition. Alcohol was only a symptom. The causes and conditions of our fatal malady were revealed to us in Steps Four and Five. The fatality of our thinking, as it relates to our drinking, is uncovered, and now we are ready for God to take away the defective thinking that leads back to the bottle.

For the alcoholic, to drink is to die! We learn that our defects of character are the fuel for the engine obsession, and we must be rid of them if we expect to live long and happily in this world. So we pray that God remove the defects of character He deems useless to His plan for our sober life. If we are still clinging to something, we simply pray for the willingness to be willing to let go. Unfortunately, it is only when the pain of holding onto our defect of character exceeds the pain of change that we become willing to let it go.

Often, our lack of willingness is caused by the fear of the unknown, and that fear keeps us clinging to the damaging defect. So we pray many times each day—"God take away this fear and direct my attention to what you would have me be."

When we place our focus on God, we outgrow our fear. The greater reliance on this prayer, the greater our potential for spiritual growth. Such is the nature of spiritual progress for the alcoholic. We don't necessarily pray for the release from pain, but release from our willfulness that keeps us clinging to the source of the pain. Most of all, we pray for freedom from self-will. This, above all, is the proper use of prayer."

We listen with open ears and an open heart

Oldtimer said, "When the we ask the newcomer to listen with an open mind, we have a responsibility to speak with an open heart. Our demonstration with the truth about our failure to control our drinking, and the success we found living the Alcoholics Anonymous way of life, are a powerful attraction to the sick and suffering alcoholic. In this way do we offer a welcome into the fellowship of the spirit.

AA is a fellowship that places honesty above image. We do not place much stock in how we look when we openly share our story, for it was a far worse experience living it than telling it. But why should we wish to shut the door on our past. It is not where live, nor is it who we are today. As a result of our rigorous honesty, a new world has opened up to us—the World of the Spirit. We have been reborn into a new way of life, and it is this vision that we offer to the newcomer.

We are a testament to the fact that God opened the gates of Alcoholic Hell, led us to the fellowship of AA, and introduced us to a program that brings much of Heaven into our lives. Once we take residence in the World of the Spirit, we awaken a Teachable Spirit within us and use the wreckage of our past to carry an effective message to the newcomer. We do not regret our past, nor do we wish to shut the door on it, for we have been blessed with a way of life that turns the trash of our past into the treasure of the present. We transform lead to gold when we open our hearts and lives to the sick and suffering alcoholic. When we do so, we find peace with the wreckage of our past, and we are able to avoid recreating such wreckage in our present.

When we enter the World of the Spirit, we interact in an entirely different manner with the world and the people about us. We no longer take from others, but give of ourselves abundantly, for God has granted us life in abundance. And now it is in giving that we receive. We were a lover of things and a user of people, but in the World of the Spirit, our self-seeking behavior dissipates. And as our fears fall from us, we learn to love God's creations as our own, and we bring peace and harmony, rather than conflict, chaos, and confusion into the lives of those we meet." We cease fighting anything and anyone, for we suddenly realize that we are among the most richly blessed of God's creations."

Alcohol did to us what we would never do to ourselves

Oldtimer said, "Just as we can act our way into a new way of thinking, we can act our way into a new way of drinking. When we reject God's way of life, we are accepting alcohols way of death. And if nothing changes, nothing changes. We remain a victim of the merciless obsession that dooms us to drink ourselves into alcoholic oblivion.

Drinking wasn't a habit or a hobby for us. It was a way of life. Alcohol brought something magical to our lives. The sensation was so overwhelming that even as it devastated our life, we turned to the bottle, time and time again, seeking relief from the problems drinking created in our life.

When we drank alcohol, we were amazed before we were halfway through with the first drink. When we drank, we knew a new freedom and a new happiness. When we drank, we did not regret the past, nor wish to shut the door on it. When we drank, we comprehended the word serenity and we knew peace. When we drank, we saw how our experience could benefit others. When we drank, that feeling of uselessness and self-pity disappeared. When we drank, we lost interest in selfish things and gained interest in our fellows. When we drank, self-seeking slipped away. When we drank, our whole attitude and outlook upon life changed. When we drank, fear of people and insecurity left us. When we drank, we intuitively knew how to handle situations that used to baffle us. When we drank, we suddenly realized that alcohol was doing for us what we could never do for ourselves.

Is this an extravagant experience? If you are alcoholic, you surely think not! These corrupt promises became our reality. We worked for this low-level spiritual experience, and alcohol became our god. We were served alcohol and had a rearrangement of ideas, emotions, and attitudes that made everything in our lives magical. In the end, we served alcohol and our ideas were corrupted, our emotions were devastated, and our attitude became self-centered. The magic had become voodoo. We lived to drink, and drank to live. Alcohol gave us wings then took away the sky.

This is an experience with alcohol that separated us from the temperate drinker, who could take alcohol or leave it alone. We could not! They could use self-will, self-knowledge, reason, and common sense to moderate their drinking or stop altogether. We could not! If given good reason, ill-health, change of environment, or the warning of a doctor, they could exercise human power and stop drinking. Not so for the alcoholic the AA founders describe in the Big Book. We have drank ourselves into a state of being that placed us beyond human aid. We have gone far down the alcoholic creek, and we are without a paddle.

When the flimsy reed of AA approached, and we grasped hold of it as a drowning man grasps a life preserver, we found ourselves on firm ground, and before us opened a pathway to a new and wonderful life. If we follow directions and take the actions AA prescribes, our thinking changes our actions. And as we continue to take the actions AA prescribes, our thinking is placed on a much higher plane, and the sky that alcohol took away reappears as we advance ever-higher into the Sunlight of the Spirit."

Our understanding of God is only the starting point of the spiritual process

Oldtimer said, "Many people attach many forms of insanity to Step Two, but the insanity it refers to is the alcoholic's inability to see and act on the truth about alcohol. The Second Step promises that God would bring forth in us the ability to see and act on the truth about alcohol by expelling the obsession for drink from our mind. We need only make the Third Step decision to live His way of life.

Many look at the Third Step and focus on "God, as you understand Him," and form a faulty interpretation of the Step Three. This off-the-wall interpretation leads them to believe they must understand God. A near impossible task that many learned, dedicated clergymen will admit that they fail to accomplish. The Third Step only requires the alcoholic to acknowledge that they have an understanding of God. Be it atheist, agnostic, or religious, this is the starting point for our pursuit of sanity through right standing with God.

As faulty or insufficient as our understanding may be, we start where we are planted, and grow a relationship with God by following the **G**ood **O**rderly **D**irections prescribed in the Steps. This brings on the next off-the-wall misunderstanding. In the Fourth Step, we are confronted with the word "moral." Right away, the alcoholic is consumed with thoughts of right and wrong. But in this instance, moral means truthful. This inventory is not about what is right or wrong, but what is true and false. It is in Step Five where we deal with right and wrong. We admit to God, ourselves, and another human being the exact nature of the wrongs we have committed as a result of our defects of character.

The unacceptable becomes acceptable in Steps Six and Seven, when we ask God to remove from us the defects that are responsible for us coming short of our philosophical convictions. We then seek to amend our wrongs and atone for our offending behavior in Steps Eight and Nine. We then continue our spiritual journey in Step Ten by continuing the inventory we started in Step Four. By clearing away the wreckage of the past, and continuing to remove the defects of character that block us from conscious contact with God, we gain access to His power. This transforms our self-centered thinking and places our thought life on the altruistic plane. We then begin to comprehend that it truly is in giving that we receive.

In Step Eleven, we seek to improve our conscious contact with God that was established in the Third Step. We receive His power through prayer and meditation, and with this power, we recover from a hopeless state of mind and body. Thus are we empowered to help other alcoholics recover from their hopeless state. This is our Twelfth Step, where we practice spiritual principles in all of our affairs, and attract other alcoholics to adopt our way of life as a solution to their malady."

Our understanding of God must be our understanding and no one else's!

Oldtimer said, "God is in us, and we are in God as the ocean is in the wave, and the wave is in the ocean. Only by accepting God as we understand God can we be true to ourselves. It is only in being true to ourselves that we can truly experience God and be of maximum service to Him and our fellow man.

To some religious-minded people, God, as we understand God, is an affront to His Divinity. It is as if we are creating God out of thin air. But in truth, it is an acknowledgement of the basic truth of the relationship between God and man. God, as we understand God, refers to our personal understanding as an atheist, agnostic or religious alcoholic. We don't have to understand God, but we each have our own personal understanding of God that we must acknowledge as truth if we are to grow in our spiritual life.

From the dawn of history, mankind has operated on a limited understanding of God. Every culture has produced a dominant idea of that relationship. However, each individual, through their own moral autonomy, has come to accept that idea based on their own self-preservation. From person to person the priority of the God idea changes to meet their circumstance. To some, God is provider. To others, God is a comforter. To others, God is a protector. To others, He is inconsequential. To others, He is nothing.

In each of these instances, people adjust their understanding based on their particular need at any specific time. For the sick and suffering alcoholic, our self-preservation is at the most basic level. God is everything, or He is nothing. That is our choice once we find ourselves at the turning point. If we expect to recover, we must accept the God idea without reservation. And according to our need, does He provide for us. He may provide knowledge when we are confused. He may provide love when we are lonely. He may be a guide when we are lost. But, ultimately, we must accept that all power resides in God. And if we are to be successful in our pursuit of sobriety, we must accept His will over our own. For we have placed ourselves beyond human aid with our obsessive pursuit of oblivion, afforded us by alcohol. Now, we are in need of the miraculous, and only through the power of the Divine do we find the means to bring that miracle about.

God is everything when we are at our bottom. This must be our understanding if we expect to live long and happily in this world. If He is nothing to us, then we are truly lost.

In AA, we find our true self when we are true to God. It is through His amazing grace that we recover and carry a sweet sound to those who seek salvation from their own alcoholic destruction."

Step Four is a spiritual exercise of self examination

Oldtimer said, "Inventory is often mistaken for a purely psychological exercise where we discover patterns of behavior that need to be changed if we hope to remain sober. It is much more than that. It is an exercise in spiritual psychotherapy, where we invite God into our brokenness that we may work with Him to bring healing to our brokenness, and amend what we have broken in others.

After our Third Step decision, we launch into the required house cleaning and invite God into the process. To not do so would turn this vital Step into another exercise in self-will—the very thing that led to our defeat. Before we put pen to paper, we pray and ask God to help us with our inventory. As alcoholics, we have a dishonest mind that can't be trusted to reveal the most damning secrets we hold. So we pray throughout the process.

In Step Four we learn the fundamentals of selfless prayer and meditation. We admit our wrongs to God through the required prayers for our resentment and fears. We seek right relations with God and our transgressors when we pray the resentment prayer: "This is a sick person. How can I be helpful to them? God save me from being angry. Thy will be done."

In doing this, we put ourselves on equal footing with our transgressors by acknowledging that they, like ourselves, are spiritually sick. We then commit ourselves to their healing. We put out of our minds the wrongs they have done, and we go to them in a helpful, forgiving spirit. As we do so, we find our own healing in God's forgiveness, and His peace overcomes our anger.

We further our right relations with God when we pray: "God take away my fear and direct my attention to what you would have me be." Rather than acting on our fears through our fight and flight instincts, we release ourselves to His calming Spirit. Through this act of faith, we outgrow our fear and find the courage to do God's will, even in the face of our fears.

When our fears fall from us, we feel the nearness of His Spirit, and through meditation, He communicates His will for us. In prayer, we offer ourselves to God to remove from us the defects of character that keep us blocked off from the power that we need in order to live up to our moral and philosophical convictions. And with this power, we go to our fellow man, repairing the wreckage of the past brought about by our insistence on living life with self-will. Thus do we fit ourselves to provide maximum service to mankind through God's will, as our actions are now guided by prayer and meditation. Through continuous conscious contact with God, we lose contact with our desire for self-destruction through alcohol, and begin a life of reconstruction as agents for God who are empowered to advance His creation."

Shame is a magnification of guilt

Guilt is an affliction that requires great energy to manage. Shame is a magnification of guilt. Whereas guilt touches our mind and clouds it in darkness, shame pierces our heart, turns it dark, and fills the alcoholic with self-loathing. We keep to ourselves the acts which bring about guilt and shame. We dare not bring them to the light of the day for fear of further rejection. In holding secret what we intuitively know is wrong, we expend great psychic energy keeping what was done in darkness away from the light. This energy we expend keeping our secrets locked within is the very psychic energy we need to recover from a hopeless state of mind and body. This is why our secrets keep us sick. And if we stay sick for too long, we will eventually drink. And for the alcoholic, to drink is to die. So our secrets not only keep us sick, they devour us and, in the end, kill us.

In Step Five, we reveal these secrets to God, ourselves, and another human being. As a result, we lose our guilt and shame, and experience forgiveness, humility, and acceptance. We lose the fear of discovery, and we begin to feel the nearness of our Creator in the release of the psychic energy that has been dammed up behind a great wall of darkness. We feel the burden of these secrets lifted from us, and we now have the power to affect a personality change within us.

But this is only in proportion to our willingness to continue to change. Through our Fifth Step experience, faith is no longer belief without proof, but trust without reservation. This newfound faith launch us into Steps Six and Seven, with an attitude of willingness and acceptance that is exhibited in our action with Steps Eight and Nine. Our acceptance of our dark secrets leads to a willingness to change our character by setting right the wrongs that have created the guilt and shame in our mind and heart, which keeps us retreating from the Light of the World.

As we make progress with amends, that light shines brighter in our life, and we understand that this is the Light of Love that is the essence of God. We are transformed by this Spirit of Life, and begin a new way of living under the Sunlight of the Spirit."

Awakening the teachable Spirit

Oldtimer said, "Step Six and Seven are essential lessons that teach us how to effectively apply Steps Ten and Eleven to our lives. In Step Six, we develop the willingness to change. If we are not willing, we pray for the willingness to be willing to change. This brings about a new relationship with pain. When the pain of staying the same becomes greater than the pain of change, we become willing to change. Thus does pain become the taproot of our spiritual growth. We let go of the source of our pain, and let God take us to better things.

In Step Seven, we pursue perfect spiritual ideas. In doing so, we will fall short of perfection, but this will reveal our shortcomings, the defects of character that block us off from God's will. We let go of the guilt, shame, regret, and remorse that lies on the axis of our perception of good and bad or right and wrong. We let God bring forth in us a Teachable Spirit that helps us correct our perception and view our mistakes as opportunities for spiritual growth.

In this teachable state, we are better aligned with the spiritual world, and work to remove the mistakes in perception that feed the ego. We accept the changes in our behavior that will reinforce the Spirit. With this heightened state of spiritual awareness, we become much more sensitive to our selfishness, dishonesty, resentment, and fear. This brings forth the pain that makes us much more willing to release our defects of character and embrace God's will as the best course of action to follow.

As this change occurs, our prayers for relief from the bondage of self are much more effective, and we undergo a spiritual growth spurt that alters our perception and reaction to life. The Teachable Spirit within unites with our mind, and we perceive eternity itself, as well as our place in it. This alters our value system, and we invest more in that which is eternal—the World of the Spirit—and much less in that which is limited—the material world in which the ego thrives. For it has been our solitary pursuit of material goals that has caused us to Ease God Out.

In Steps Six and Seven, we accept our role as agents for God and our motivations change, as does our perception, which leads to the choices that determine the actions we take in life. Now, we perceive our past harms to others as the stairway we ascend, amends by amends, to achieve a new life in the fourth dimension of existence."

From the God idea to a relationship with God

Oldtimer said, "Step Three was a decision to commit our thinking and actions to God. In Step Seven, we commit our heart to our Creator. We lay aside our burdens and allow him to level our load. We carry only what is useful to Him, and only for as long as He would have us carry it. Our job is to accept ourselves as we are, and keep our feet on the road to a happy destiny. We find that His yoke is easy, and His burden light. God doesn't ask more of us than we are able to carry with His assistance. Where He guides, He provides. So we trust God will provide what we need to meet the daily challenges our spiritual life brings.

By living life on God's terms, we are easily able to live life on life's terms. We find that in every difficult situation, we receive a blessing or a lesson. We fully recognize that of ourselves we are nothing. With self-will we added nothing to life, but subtracted God's grace from our life. By living in God's will, we multiply His grace until it overflows from our life, into the lives of others we encounter in His world. Thus do we demonstrate His omnipotence in all of our affairs.

Before we came to AA we knew not God. Instead, we worked with a God idea given to us by someone else. Recognition of this was sufficient to begin the transformation necessary for us to launch into recovery. By uncovering, discovering, and discarding the things within us that blocked God from entering our lives, we came to experience the presence of our Creator.

In Step Seven, we allow God to do the work of spiritual transformation. We need only commit to His way of life and remain useful to our fellow man. In doing so, we demonstrate His omnipotence. Through self-will, we ran our life into the ground. We brought great harm to others while seeking our comfort. If we are to continue to receive God's redeeming grace, we must be hard on ourselves and considerate of others. Such a change in perspective is essential if we are to go forth with the rest of the program.

We created every problem in our life with our distorted thinking. When God enters our heart, He transforms our thinking, and selflessness becomes the mortar that binds the stones we use to reconstruct our lives."

We are not our mistakes

Oldtimer said, "It is not our mistakes that ultimately determine our identity. It is how we correct our mistakes that defines who we are.

We caused untold harm to the people who entered our lives. As such, we became a weapon of mass destruction formed against ourselves. If we are to heal from our self-inflicted wounds, we must take the lead to correct our mistakes and offer others the healing we seek.

Our mistakes do not make us bad people. We are sick people with a mental illness known as alcoholism, which drove us to harm others, especially those we loved most. This caused self-loathing and shame within us. A major part of the insanity of alcoholism is the shame we internalize for what we have done to others. Guilt is the natural reaction to harming others, but as a people who are enslaved to their emotional nature, we take the extreme position of shame as an identity. And with this identification, we deem ourselves unworthy of God's grace, and accept a condemnation He does not desire for us.

Our escape from the emotional and psychological prison in which we have locked ourselves lies in the direct amends to those we have harmed, and a change in the behavior that brought about the harm. When we do so, we usually change the perception the aggrieved party has of us. If their perception doesn't change, then we change our own perception of ourselves and move out of the shadow of shame, and step higher into the Sunlight of the Spirit. As we bask in the glow of the Spirit, we come to love ourselves unconditionally and realize the purity of our essential nature as a spiritual being.

Our human experience has taken the low road through alcoholism, but now it rises to the a higher plane of altruistic living where we give of ourselves to our fellow man. And as we do so we are filled with the Spirit and project the love we receive to those we encounter on a daily basis. For giving to receive is the essence of the spiritual life for the self-centered alcoholic. We give because we owe. And as we continue to give we we continue to grow. And as we grow we owe. So we give because we owe.

A change in behavior is the best apology

Oldtimer said, "The best apology we offer those we have harmed requires a change in behavior. This is the proper amends we must make to atone to those we have wronged. Without a change in behavior, we are merely manipulating our victim for another fall. A simple apology will suffice if we have harmed someone by acting out of character. But when we repeatedly act out on a character defect, such as dishonesty or unselfishness, making amends is necessary. We must not only be prepared to offer an apology and make restitution where needed, we must also be willing to change our behavior so that we no longer act out on the same defect of character with different people. To do so is nothing more than dishonesty.

Our old behavior stems from our old ideas, emotions, and attitude that supported our alcoholic life. And though we may have had a spiritual awakening that removed our obsession for drinking, we must make the necessary changes in our behavior, where indicated by our inventory and our newly awakened Spirit. Our inventory revealed that we were selfish, dishonesty, and inconsiderate in our relationships. We now act our way into a new way of thinking with a new approach toward life where we are hard on ourselves and considerate of others. This new behavior may not be in harmony with our feelings, so if it doesn't feel right, we do the next right thing and apply the principles of the program to the problem. We pray for the right thought or right action, and the power to act upon the guidance provided.

The principles of the Four Absolutes, a long forgotten practice of the Oxford Group, will often reveal our shortcomings and guide us to the next right action. Purity—is it ugly or beautiful? Unselfishness—how does it affect the other person? Honesty—is it true or is it false? Love—is it right or wrong?

These Absolutes reveal the shortcomings of our emotions and guide our prayer life, as we seek God's help in our transformation from old to new. And as we practice the principles of the program in all of our affairs, this spiritual habit takes root and becomes our new nature!"

We are transformed by the Spirit when we live the Steps

Oldtimer said, "When we are in bondage to self, we often find ourselves as hostage to the whims of other people. Their actions ignite an impulse from our instincts for sex, society and security, and we feel compelled to react. The response generally takes the form of self-seeking behavior, where we attempt to rearrange the external situation to fix our internal discomfort. In this way, we are transformed by the world. The ways of the world determine whether we are happy or sad, elated or depressed, peaceful or angry, etc. Only by living according to spiritual principles can we avoid becoming a hostage to the whims of other people.

When we live the AA program, we allow ourselves to be transformed by the Spirit by removing the barriers in our character that act against God's will. We watch for the manifestation of self that responds to every slight against us. When selfishness, dishonesty, resentment, and fear guide our actions, it separates us from God. And the further we move from God, the closer we move towards the first drink.

So when we are offended, we take advantage of our new partnership with our Creator and ask Him to remove the defect of character we are tempted to respond with.

Resentment is the number one offender. An ounce of forgiveness spares us a ton of misery when others bring pain into our lives. Instead of responding with anger to the pain, we ask God for the wisdom to know the source of our pain, and the understanding of our antagonist's pain as well.

Hurt people hurt people. This axiom has been in play since Cain slew Able for the slight he felt from God. When in bondage to self, we can go so far as to have murderous intentions for others. For most humans, this crosses a line that they are not willing to cross. But some actually cross the line with terrible deeds. Perhaps we only seek to slay someones character with words, but the ruinous words are like an acid that does more damage to the one that holds it than the one for whom it is intended. And with the alcoholic, whose hope is the growth and maintenance of a spiritual life, the results can be deadly.

Bondage to self is a luxury for normal men and women. We can ill-afford such luxury. Instead, we offer prayer for those who have harmed us, just as we would a sick friend. But most importantly, we offer forgiveness for their actions. For, through understanding ourselves, we come to understand others, and forgiveness comes easily when we realize that they, like us, know not what they do when in bondage to self."

Lack of prayer is our dilemma

Oldtimer said, "Lack of power is our dilemma. We rely on self-will to live the life we desire, but it only leads us back to alcohol and a life we do not desire. For the alcoholic, a life run on self-will can hardly be a success. If we are to live successfully sober, the proper use of self-will lies in exerting it toward the application of the Steps in all of our affairs. In order to accomplish this task, inventory, prayer, and meditation are a requirement.

Through inventory, we learn where our life has been out of alignment with God's will. Thus, we lack the power to see and act on the truth about alcohol. Nor do we have the power to live up to our moral and philosophical convictions. So we identify the manifestations of self-will that have led to our defeat, and in prayer we surrender them to God.

In the Third Step, we accepted our role as agents for God. This prayer was only the beginning of a lifetime of transformation that prepares us for maximum service to God and His world.

Through inventory, we found that we served a lower power with our attachment to selfishness, dishonesty, resentment, and fear. These bedevilments fueled our alcoholic life and kept us in bondage to alcohol, our lower power. When we uncovered these manifestations in our life, we prayed for God to remove them. We then meditated on God's will for us in each matter where our defects of character have brought harm to others. This is the proper use of prayer. "Thy will, not mine," is expressed in every Step we take. And as we proceed through the program, we are fitting ourselves to become prayer warriors, who change the world by changing themselves.

Prayer always changes the one who prays. It is the medium of miracles from the One who has all power to the one who properly prays. With each prayer, we discard the manifestation of self that no longer holds any value to the spiritual structure through which we walk through to freedom. As we trudge our way to a happy destiny, we stop frequently and pray, "Thy will, not mine, be done." Thus do we continue to improve upon our conscious contact with our Creator as He removes every defect of character that stands in the way of our usefulness to Him and our fellow man.

When He reveals His will for us, He grants us the power to carry it out. And so long as we remain in alignment with Him, our will and His will are one."

Letting go of old ideas brings forth a new freedom and a new happiness

Oldtimer said, "We find much of Heaven when we trudge the road to happy destiny. We existed in a hopeless state of mind and body that led us down the road to perdition. The Twelve Steps redirected us from a path that led to insanity and death, and put us on the road to a fourth dimension of existence in the World of the Spirit. We feel as though God opened the gates of Heaven and let us in, but in reality, He opened the gates of Hell and let us out.

We found that exiting Alcoholic Hell is a heavenly experience where we realized a new freedom and a new happiness. The new freedom is not merely release from the bondage to alcohol, but release from our bondage to the irrational thinking that led to our maniacal drinking. We were enslaved to alcohol, and often drank against our will. In this dark world, we were held in bondage to the insanity of selfishness, which doomed us to repeat the same mistakes over and over again while expecting a different result. We

Eased **G**od **O**ut and suffered the pain and humiliation that alcohol repeatedly delivered. We suffered as a slave to our emotional nature, which left us restless, irritable and discontented when we ceased drinking. Such was the nature of the alcoholic dilemma that made our human existence hellish indeed.

By following **G**ood **O**rderly **D**irections, we are released from our enslavement to alcohol, and find a new way of life that gets infinitely more wonderful as time passes. Our bondage to the insane self-centered emotions and ideas that made our lives unmanageable expires, and we aspire to a greater Self, where the joy of living manifests in all of our affairs. We seek God's will over our human instincts for sex, society, and security and as a result, we are in much less danger of fear, anger, worry, self-pity, and foolish decisions. For we become fertile soil in which spiritual seeds are planted and bring forth a harvest of virtuous behavior. We are full of faith, hope, charity, love, patience, forgiveness, and compassion for our fellows. We send out these good vibrations, and they are returned to us in great abundance.

Whereas we once drove away those about us, we now become a beacon that attracts the lost, lonely souls of alcoholics who desperately seek the happy, joyous and free life we now possess."

A choice for that restores

Oldtimer said, "Step One is all about choice and control when it comes to alcohol. There are people who can choose not to drink. Unlike the alcoholic, who has lost the power of choice and control, they don't drink under any circumstances, if they so desire. And should they choose to drink, they can control how much they drink. Not so with the alcoholic, who has lost the power of choice and control over the drink.

AA allows each individual to diagnose themselves and determine if they are the type of drinker that can exercise choice and control over alcohol, or are they the type who has lost the power of choice and control. We, who are constitutionally incapable of controlling how much we drink once we start, and are mentally incapacitated to come to a logical conclusion concerning the impact alcohol has on their lives, need a power greater than human power to recover from an inhuman condition.

The gates of insanity and death await the alcoholic who continues to drink in spite of the pain, suffering and humiliation that comes from their maniacal pursuit of the pleasure alcohol once delivered. This type is so blinded by the past pleasure of the drink that they can no longer see and act on the truth about alcohol. This is the root of the insane thinking that twists our mental faculties into an intense, anguished defense of our insane drinking habit.

Alcohol did something wonderful for us when we first picked it up. It was a magical elixir that delivered a bliss to life, and solved our main problem—life on life's terms. Over time, the script flipped and alcohol started doing something *to us*, rather than *for us*. But in our delusional mind, we were convinced that it was still doing for us what we could not do for ourselves. This belief was the beginning of a delusional thought life that placed us beyond human aid. We were in full flight from reality and focused only of the past pleasure alcohol brought us. As a result, we trained our mind to focus on the pleasures of a long—gone past, and avoid the pain of our dysfunctional present. In doing so, our lives became unmanageable. We grew maladjusted to life and lost our vision of a bright future.

The magic of alcohol turned into voodoo and cursed us with terror, bewilderment, frustration, and despair! Alcohol had become a cruel task-master that sought to destroy our lives, and the lives of our loved ones, at every turn and in every fashion. We had a master that served us not. A master that promised us the gift of flight, and then took away the sky.

In AA, we found we had a new choice. A choice to live on a spiritual basis and turn control over to the One who has all power. Thus do we find a new Master, who rescues us from our self-imposed destruction, and brings a new freedom and a new happiness into our life and the lives of our loved ones. He provides what we need to live happy, joyous and free, so long as we keep close to Him and follow the Steps to a bright future and existence in the spiritual dimension of life. A life more abundant than any we could have delivered ourselves. He does for us what no human power could accomplish— deliver us from the evil that is alcoholism. Under His care, we find a new way of life that becomes infinitely more wonderful as time passes, and grants us the power to deliver this miracle to others who serve under the lash of alcohol."

A rude awakening at our bottom precedes our spiritual awakening

Oldtimer said, "Much is said in meetings about hitting bottom. The bottom differs greatly for every alcoholic. Some alcoholics have to be badly mangled before they fully accept the truth of their condition. This is the rude awakening that precedes a spiritual awakening that manifests in many different forms.

A high-bottom alcoholic is one who sees the bottom of the alcoholic pit coming before they actually hit it. A low-bottom alcoholic is one who has to splash on the bottom of the pit before they believe it exists. Either way, an alcoholic can be said to hit bottom when they come to believe in the hopelessness and futility of life as they had been living it, and reject the idea that somehow, someday, they will once again control and enjoy their drinking.

This idea of controlling alcohol doesn't occur in the average temperate drinker. They can take it or leave it alone. However, it is the great obsession of every alcoholic. The persistence of this illusion is astonishing. Many alcoholics pursue it to the gates of insanity, or the ultimate bottom—death. When we become willing to pick up the kit of spiritual tools AA offers, and follow the path of those who have solved the drink problem, it can be said we have hit the bottom. Thus do we smash the idea that we are like others who can safely drink. We destroy this idea by inducing an entire psychic change within us. By following the clear-cut, precise, exact directions the AA program offers, we undergo an entire rearrangement of ideas, emotions, and outlook upon God's world.

The bottom teaches us lessons we could never attain on the highest mountaintop. It serves as our launching point to freedom from our obsession for maniacal drinking. And upon the rubble of our ruinous obsession for alcohol, we build a wonderful spiritual structure through which we trudge the road to a happy destiny."

Two mental conclusions lead to a decision

Old timers said, "Steps One and Two are simultaneous mental conclusions we make upon entering the rooms of recovery. When we arrive in AA we are presented with a diagnosis of our physical and mental state. This diagnosis brands us as hopeless alcoholics. If we accept the diagnosis, we come back to our second meeting ready to make a life-altering decision. If not, we delay the decision. Either way, we make a decision.

If we make a decision to reject the solution to our problem, then we obviously do not fully comprehend the fatal nature of our illness. Furthermore, we do not understand the faulty thinking upon which our mind operates. We may take some more convincing—either by continuing to come to meetings and using all manner of self-deception and experimentation to prove we are not alcoholics in need spiritual help, or by returning to our drinking habit, hoping against hope that we are not truly alcoholic. We convince ourselves that next time, our drinking will be different. We believe that we have the power to control how much we drink, and can avoid the consequences that always follow our drunken sprees.

This denial of reality is rooted in our cognitive dissonance. We so deeply believe in our limited human power because we have used it in the past to solve other difficult problems. To surrender to the conclusions of Steps One and Two feels like death to the alcoholic ego. In truth, that is exactly what it is! When a psychic change occurs, the alcoholic ego dies off and we give birth to our Divine Mind, which contains the power to break the hold alcohol has over us. This birth is difficult and full of psychic pain, and there are many who pay the high price of this disease rather than humble themselves and accept the AA solution. They would rather die believing they were right, than admit they were wrong and live life happy, joyous and free.

This is a perfect example of the deadly pride that an alcoholic brings into the rooms of recovery and carries to the grave with them if they do not find the humility that recovery requires. To survive our fatal malady, we must humble ourselves to the truth in Steps One and Two, and make the decision in Step Three to further humble ourselves and turn our will and our lives over to the care and direction of a loving and merciful God. For what we alcoholics need more than anything else is love and mercy. Our actions indicate a sincere self-loathing, which leads to our destruction. The fellowship provides us with the unconditional love that we lack, and the Steps grant us the mercy of God's grace, which spares us our fatal fate as alcoholics.

His grace delivers us to a way of life far beyond anything we felt we deserved. Our choice is to get busy living or get busy dying. We can accept spiritual help, do the required hard work, and reap the abundant harvest God has stored away for us. Or we can continue our hard drinking and accept our fate of jails, institutions and death, which our disease has stored for us. Choose wisely. Choose life.

Inventory is a look at life from an entirely different angle

Oldtimer said, "Until one understands perspective, there can be no objectivity. Until one obtains objectivity, there can be no peace of mind.

The alcoholic's perspective is rooted in self-centeredness. The Fourth Step forces us to take an objective view of our life. We continue to watch for self-centeredness throughout our sober life.

We must fit ourselves to be of maximum service to God and our fellows, because we are a black hole of selfishness that will suck the life out of others, and eventually ourselves. This malady is a subtle foe. We feel comfortable with self-centeredness, and will often rationalize, justify and minimize our selfish behavior. But we, as alcoholics, cannot afford the luxury of selfishness. We must be rid of it or it will kill us. Our very lives may depend on the constant thought of others. So we must watch for the rationalization, justification, and minimization of our behavior.

When we are in God's will, there isn't a need for such mental gymnastics. We must constantly turn back to our inventory, for it holds the key to our future. We must be prepared to look at every situation from an entirely different angle. The alcoholic is naturally self-seeking. We are like the actor trying to run the whole show—forever trying to arrange the lights, the scenery, the ballet, and the rest of the players in his own way. If only his arrangements would stay put, if only people would do as he wished, the show would be great. Everybody, including himself, would be pleased. Life would be wonderful.

This perspective is what makes our life unmanageable. We are forever trying to arrange the outer world to bring peace to our inner world. It doesn't work, and we become angry, indignant, and self-pitying, until we develop a fatal case of the Poor Me's—Poor me, poor me, pour me a drink.

Acceptance is the answer to the problem of the self-seeking alcoholic. This is the perspective that frees us from the negative forces in our mind that seek to pull us down and keep us down. We have to accept that not everyone will see the world, or situations in the world, as we do. Our biggest obstacle to peace of mind is our childish, self-centered insistence that others see the world through our perspective. Objectivity is the adult response to these differences. When others disagree with us, it's not the end of the world. It is just their perspective, and we must allow them to have it. After all, we have to quit playing God. It doesn't work.

When we complain about people, places, things, or situations, we are complaining about God's handiwork. We are saying that we know better than God how His world should operate. It is only by God's grace that we did not get what we deserved, instead we are blessed to receive a chance at a way of life that satisfies all of our needs and most of our wants. Yet we quite often sulk, whine, and childishly insist on more. This self-pity is the drug we take before we take a drink. An attitude of gratitude is a requirement for happy contented sobriety, and this comes from a new perspective that allows us to objectively view God's world and His people. So long as we live to serve God, His people will provide us the lessons we need to grow our spiritual life."

Confession sets us free from the falsehoods that hold us in bondage

Oldtimer said, "The truth will set you free. But before it can, you need to know exactly what lie is holding you hostage. The big lie that held us hostage, and exacted a high ransom for our release, was the lie we told ourselves about alcohol. We believed it was doing something *for* us, when in fact, it was doing something *to* us—destroying us one drink at a time.

This lie overrode our most powerful instinct. That of survival. Once we overcome it, we are faced with the more subtle lies we hold about our instincts for sex, society, and security. If we were willing to sacrifice our life to support a lie that was killing us, how deep must be our deception about what we need. These subtle lies keep us in bondage to self-will, the antithesis to God's will. Only through rigorous honesty can we uncover the lies that we have for so long mistaken for the gospel truth. With each layer of falsehood we expose to the light of inventory, we find a greater degree of freedom from bondage to the ideas, emotions, and attitudes that work against our spiritual development. We can only experience spiritual growth to the extent that we embrace the truth about ourselves. The ugly truth we uncover allows us to discover the hidden beauty that is our spiritual essence.

For every fear we release, we find a greater level of freedom. We find that behind the **F**alse **E**vidence **A**ppearing **R**eal was a courage we did not know we possessed. It revealed itself only when we exercised the simple act of pursuing the truth. Every resentment reveals an integrity in the beliefs we hold. If we passionately defend that which will destroy us, how much greater will our passion for forgiveness grow when we discover its true benefits? When we discover that giving is truly receiving, how richly charitable shall we become? When we confess the truth of our bondage to our defects of character, we discard the falsehoods that blind us to the truth of God's love for us. Now, so much deeper shall be our commitment to serve Him?

Identifying our falsehoods requires the key of willingness to walk the path of truth, holding nothing sacred but truth itself. In fact, we seek not God, but the truth, and in the truth we find God. Only our pride blocks the pathway to true happiness, which awaits our arrival in the fourth dimension of existence. When we humbly lay aside our desire to be right, and accept the error of our ways, we begin to build a life that gets infinitely more wonderful as time passes."

Humility is the Spirit of Steps Six and Seven

Oldtimer said, "When we live fully in the spirit of Steps Six and Seven, it can truly be said that we have been restored to our right standing with God. We have become willing to humble ourselves before God, and have Him remove from us the defects of character which stand in the way of our usefulness to Him. We know who we are and Whose we are. No longer are we in full flight from reality, seeking to arrange life to suit our purpose. No longer do we act out on old behavior and expect a different result. We recognize that self-will always produces the same disastrous results in sobriety that it produced in our drunkenness. We recognize that our old behaviors produce the same old results, and so long as we remain willing to change, we can fail our way to success as we trudge toward the happy destiny God has ordained for those who earnestly seek Him.

Our Teachable Spirit has awakened, and we prosper on the spiritual level with every failure we encounter on the material level. Each experience bears a gift. It is either a lesson, a blessing, or both. Truth is no longer a weapon to be feared, but a tool by which we uncover, discover, and discard the manifestations of self that block us from God's grace.

Scripture says, no weapon formed against you can prosper. This holds true for those who seek to enlarge and perfect their spiritual life. When we have a spiritual awakening, we join a Fellowship of the Spirit, which stretches back to the dawn of man. Alcoholics are not the only ones who have experienced a spiritual awakening. This has been happening since the dawn time. But no one has ever needed this experience more than the alcoholic. Without it, we perish!

So we humbly submit our will and life to God's care, and we live His way of life to the best of our ability. In doing so, we are not only restored to sanity, but empowered by the Sunlight of the Spirit to grow in the image of our Creator as we develop a life based on humility, peace, wisdom, love, and courage."

When we Ease God Out we lose serenity, courage and wisdom

Oldtimer said, "The alcoholic ego is a force in our mind that is aligned with our disease. It gives birth to a hundred forms of fear, self-delusion, self-seeking, and self-pity that makes our lives unmanageable and drives our obsession for alcohol.

Steps Six and Seven prepare us for battle against the alcoholic ego. Having taken hold of the truth in Steps Four and Five, we adopt attitudes that allow us to address the wrongs we have uncovered by making amends to those we have harmed. Step Six is an acknowledgement that we can do nothing to remove our defects of character, other than adopt a willingness to have God remove them—a willingness that grows through the pain that living by self-will creates.

In Step Seven, we accept that we are fatally flawed, and that we will continue to harm others if we allow the alcoholic ego to drive us. In opposition to the self-centered alcoholic ego is maximum service to others. Rather than Ease God Out and pursue our selfish motives, demands, and desires, we seek to play the role God assigns. We give of ourselves to others without an expectation of return. As a result, God grants us serenity, courage and wisdom to meet calamity with serenity.

As we feel His power flow in, we enjoy peace of mind. And in this peace does the alcoholic ego lose it's dominance over our mind. Our fears fall from us as our faith increases. Through our faith, our emotional wounds are healed and the obsession to drink is lifted. No longer are we restless, irritable, and discontented, and seeking comfort in alcohol. Instead, we find comfort in sobriety, and we cease fighting anything and anyone—even alcohol. The problem has been removed, and in the clarity of thought that is God's wisdom, we are strengthened and are easily able surmount the obstacles before us on the path to a happy destiny."

Amends requires a change in our behavior

Oldtimer said, "The best apology is a change in behavior. This is the essence of the amends we must make to those we have wronged, and to ourselves if we expect to live long and happily in this world. A simple apology will suffice if we have simply harmed someone by acting out of character. But when we repeatedly harm others by acting out on our character defect, such as selfishness, dishonesty, resentment and fear, we violate a trust and amends is necessary. We must not only be prepared to offer an apology, and make restitution where needed, we must also be willing to change our behavior so that we no longer act out on the same defect of character with different people. Doing so is nothing more than a manipulation born of dishonesty. Our old behavior stems from our old alcoholic ideas, emotions and attitude. And though we may have had a spiritual awakening that removed our obsession for drinking, we must continue to make the necessary changes in our behavior where indicated by our inventory if we are to maintain our newfound spiritual status. Our inventory revealed that we were selfish, dishonesty and inconsiderate in our relationships. In recovery we act our way into a new way of thinking with a new approach towards life where we are hard on ourselves and considerate of others. This new approach to life may not be in harmony with our feelings, so if it doesn't feel right we do the next right thing and apply the principles of the program to the problem. The guiding principles of the Four Absolutes, a long forgotten practice of the Oxford Group, will very often reveal our shortcomings to us and guide us to the next right action. Purity-Is it ugly or beautiful; Unselfish-How does it affect the other person: Honesty-Is it true or is it false: Love-Is it right or wrong. The Four Absolutes reveal our shortcomings and act as a guide in our prayer life as we seek God's help in our transformation from old to new. As we practice the principles of the program in all of our affairs, the habit of prayer takes root and becomes our nature as we trudge the road to a happy destiny."

Amends restores balance to God's world

Oldtimer said, "No justice! No peace! The alcoholic scale of justice is always weighted in favor of the alcoholic. If we were ninety-nine percent wrong and the other party was one percent wrong, in the alcoholic mind the offending party is one-hundred percent wrong. This sleight of mind is born of our inability to accept the truth about our life. Where there is no truth there is no justice, and where there is no justice there is no peace. Such is the fate of agents of alcoholic destruction. We could not see and act on the truth about alcohol, and sought to blame everything but the drink for our miserable state of affairs. Through every form of deception known to man, we denied the truth of our relationship with alcohol. This deception carried over into all of our other relationships. It is this dynamic of the alcoholic life that makes true justice an impossibility for alcoholics, and peaceful existence with our fellow man an improbability This dysfunctional approach to life left us restless, irritable and discontented, and the worry and anxiety we experienced always resulted in another drink. We eventually reached a point where chemical peace of mind, via the drink, eluded our grasp. And as our grasp on reality failed we slipped deeper into a delusional state. Only through a through a rigorous pursuit of justice could we find the peace within that we need to live a happy, productive, sober life. And only by turning our will and life over to the Author of Truth, are we able to look at our life objectively, discover the true nature of our problems and deliver a just remedy to them. In the Hopi language amends means restoring balance to the universe. We are maladjusted to the universe and in full flight from reality. Recovery requires us to make amends to ourselves by taking the recommended Steps to change our life. We make amends to God when we restore balance to His Universe by repairing the damage we inflicted upon its inhabitants. This calls for a just accounting for our actions. We put out of mind the wrongs of others entirely, and look only for our own mistakes. This negates the alcoholic scales of justice, and puts us in balance with Divine Justice. We find God does not make too hard terms with us. His Mercy insures we do not receive what we think we deserve, and His Grace insures we receive what we think we do not deserve. Such is the Divine Justice of God. We receive in greater measure than what we give. But to one whom much is given, much is also expected. So we continue to trudge the road to happy destiny and bring onto the path as many of our sick brethren as we can. For in doing so, we restore balance to the universe in a fair and just manner befitting an Agent of God."

Service to others is a labor of love

Oldtimer said, "As we continue our journey into recovery, we find that our path leads us into the World of the Spirit. We laboriously follow a path traveled by many like us who found redemption in the pain of change, and a grace we thought was beyond our worth. Each Step we took relieved us of a spiritual malady that made sober life unbearable, and another drink attractive—a drink we knew carried another engagement with terror, bewilderment, frustration, and despair.

As the storm of alcohol abated, the clouds of selfishness, dishonesty, resentment, and fear dissipated. We began to bask in the Sunlight of the Spirit, for we have removed the blocks between ourselves and God. As a result, we have come into conscious contact with the purity of our true self, and recognize that we are no longer human beings seeking a spiritual experience, but spiritual beings having a human experience. It is then that God reveals Himself to us, and our perception of the world changes, where we look upon our former enemies as spiritually sick, and our friends as kindred Spirits in the fourth dimension of existence. Our defects of character are thus transformed into the assets that God originally blessed us with before alcoholism twisted their purpose.

Faith replaces fear. Forgivenesses replaces resentment. Charity replaces selfishness. And humility takes root in our personality and allows truth to penetrate our soul and bring its healing power to bear. Thus have we prepared ourselves to maximize our service to God and fulfill our role as His agents, who bring freedom from bondage to the sick and suffering alcoholic. But this is only the beginning of the work of a lifetime. We never arrive at a spiritual plateau where we can rest. Complacency now becomes our enemy. Every day is a day we must continue to take personal inventory and promptly admit our wrongs. Every day is a day we ask God to take away our defects of character. Every day is a day we make amends with those we have harmed. Every day is a day we draw closer to God by removing the barriers that stand against His will."

Conscious contact with God transforms our mind

Oldtimer said, "Conscious contact with God means just that. When we are conscious, we should contact God. This can only happen if we practice spiritual integrity and accept God simply as we understand God. There isn't a correct answer when it comes to our understanding of God. Nor is one understanding better than another. Only the truth of our understanding counts. For it is in our pursuit of the truth that we enter into conscious contact with God. And it is this experience that defines our understanding of God as we trudge the road to a happy destiny.

When we come into the fellowship we carry the seed of our destruction as well as the seed of our resurrection. We have an alcoholic mind that paves the path to a miserable destiny at the gates of insanity and death. So long as we rely on it to guide our life, our destruction is assured. We also carry the fundamental idea about God that will guide us on our path to a happy destiny in the World of the Spirit.

We are either atheist, agnostic, or religious when we come to AA seeking relief from a fatal malady. Whatever our understanding, it is sufficient to begin the spiritual quest that insures our recovery from a fatal malady. We need only be honest, open-minded, and willing to follow **G**ood **O**rderly **D**irections. When we do so, our alcoholic mind gives way to an ever advancing God idea that begins to dominate our consciousness, and we undergo a spiritual experience that brings about a rearrangement of ideas, emotions, and attitudes that center our focus on God's will. Thus are we are blessed with a new mind that rejects the obsessive idea that drives us to embrace the way of death that alcohol provides.

This God idea requires constant maintenance. If we expect to live happy, joyous and free in recovery, we must have an open-mind towards all spiritual matters. When we do so, all matters are spiritual. Even when we look upon on our enemies, we sense the purity of their spiritual nature, which they do not yet recognize. No longer do we let them pull us into their storm. Instead, we pull them into our peace, with love, understanding and forgiveness. When we bless them with the gifts God has granted us, we transform our relationship with them, and they become the teachers of the spiritual principles we practice. They may or may not change, but our attitude and outlook upon our fellow man changes. So it is in all of our affairs. In our newfound relationship with our Creator, we trust Infinite God rather than our finite mind. In doing so, we become His happy, joyous and free agents empowered to advance His creation, one day at a time."

Transmitting what we have keeps us on God's frequency

Oldtimer said, "Those who are spiritually awakened have little interest in other's drama. After all, we have ceased fighting anything and anyone—even alcohol. We have been restored to sanity, peace has overcome our mind, and we can now maintain our focus on AA's primary purpose. By doing so, we insure that our ongoing personal journey in recovery will reach its fruition. So long as we make our peace of mind non-negotiable, our recovery remains our top priority, and our focus remains on the principles of the program that keep us balanced through life's ups and downs. We are in much less danger of excitement, fear, anger, self-pity or foolish decisions. Many conflicts and controversies will come our way to distract us from our primary spiritual aim, but with AA's kit of spiritual tools at our disposal, we can employ spiritual principles to these problems and give unto the world that which is the world's, and give unto God that which is His—our time, energy and effort.

Through the application of the Steps to our lives on a daily basis, we maintain a buoyancy in our life that allows us to rise above the troubles that come our way. We meet conflict and chaos with serenity, for we have touched eternity, and have awakened to the Great Reality within and attained a spiritual perception whereby we see God's hand in even the most tragic of situations. Our very lives become examples of God's omnipotence, and when we demonstrate a willingness to seek and do His will, we are empowered to bring unto the world the grace, and mercy it needs. Under the care and direction of God, we are able to practice AA principles in all of our affairs. So long as our spiritual aim stays true, we meet calamity with serenity, and we are able to bring love where there is hatred, forgiveness where there is injury, faith where there is doubt, hope where there is despair, joy where there is sorrow, and light where there is darkness.

In our transformation we learn that it is in giving that we receive. When we pray for knowledge of God's will for us, and the power to carry it out, we find that sobriety is God's will for us, and in helping another alcoholic through the Steps we are given the power to maintain our own sobriety."